T0181221

Advances in Information Security

Volume 67

Series editor

Sushil Jajodia, George Mason University, Fairfax, VA, USA

More information about this series at http://www.springer.com/series/5576

Ehab Al-Shaer • Mohammad Ashiqur Rahman

Security and Resiliency Analytics for Smart Grids

Static and Dynamic Approaches

 Springer

Ehab Al-Shaer
Department of Software and Information
  Systems
University of North Carolina, Charlotte
Charlotte, NC, USA

Mohammad Ashiqur Rahman
Department of Computer Science
Tennessee Tech University
Cookeville, TN, USA

ISSN 1568-2633
Advances in Information Security
ISBN 978-3-319-81389-9   ISBN 978-3-319-32871-3   (eBook)
DOI 10.1007/978-3-319-32871-3

© Springer International Publishing Switzerland 2016
Softcover reprint of the hardcover 1st edition 2016
This work is subject to copyright. All rights are reserved by the Publisher, whether the whole or part of
the material is concerned, specifically the rights of translation, reprinting, reuse of illustrations, recitation,
broadcasting, reproduction on microfilms or in any other physical way, and transmission or information
storage and retrieval, electronic adaptation, computer software, or by similar or dissimilar methodology
now known or hereafter developed.
The use of general descriptive names, registered names, trademarks, service marks, etc. in this publication
does not imply, even in the absence of a specific statement, that such names are exempt from the relevant
protective laws and regulations and therefore free for general use.
The publisher, the authors and the editors are safe to assume that the advice and information in this book
are believed to be true and accurate at the date of publication. Neither the publisher nor the authors or
the editors give a warranty, express or implied, with respect to the material contained herein or for any
errors or omissions that may have been made.

Printed on acid-free paper

This Springer imprint is published by Springer Nature
The registered company is Springer International Publishing AG Switzerland

The whole of science is nothing more than a refinement of everyday thinking.

— Albert Einstein

Preface

Driven by the rapid advancement of technology and the growing need of business requirements, cyber communications are embedded in many physical systems. The integration of cyber and physical capabilities leads to the creation of many applications with enormous societal impact and economic benefit. The emerging systems that connect the cyber-world of computing and communications with the physical world are cyber-physical systems (CPS). Operations are monitored, analyzed, and controlled in CPS using cyber systems that interconnect physical components. Many CPS are defined as critical infrastructures due to their national importance. According to the U.S. Department of Homeland Security, "Critical infrastructures are the assets, systems, or networks, whose incapacitation or destruction would have a debilitating effect on security, national economic security, national public health or safety". Any damage or unavailability of such a critical infrastructure often has a massive and broader impact.

This book targets a state-of-the-art important concern of protecting critical infrastructures like smart grids. The work presents various static and dynamic security analysis techniques that can automatically verify smart grid security and resiliency and provably identify potential attacks in a proactive manner. These techniques serve three major security and resiliency analysis objectives. The first objective is to formally verify the compliance of smart grid configurations with the security and resiliency guidelines. More specifically, a formal framework is presented that verifies the compliance of the advanced metering infrastructure and supervisory control and data acquisition system with the security and resiliency requirements, and generates remediation plans for potential security violations. The second objective is the formal verification of the security and resiliency of smart grid control systems. In this respect, a formal model is presented that analyzes attack evasions on state estimation, a core control module of the supervisory control system in smart grids. The model identifies attack vectors that can compromise state estimation. This part also includes risk mitigation techniques that formally synthesize proactive security plans that make such attacks infeasible. The last effort discusses the dynamic security analysis for smart grid. It is shown that AMI behavior can be modeled using event logs collected at smart collectors, which in turn can be verified using the specification invariants generated from the configurations of the AMI devices.

Although the focus of this book is the smart grid security and resiliency, the presented formal analytics are generic enough to be extended for other cyber-physical systems, especially which are involved with industrial control systems (ICS). Therefore, industry professionals and academic researchers will find this book as an exceptional resource to learn theoretical and practical aspects of applying formal methods for the protection of critical infrastructures.

Unlike the existing books on the smart grid security that mostly discuss various security issues and corresponding challenges, this book offers unique solutions addressing these challenges. The book covers novel techniques which can automatically, provably, and efficiently analyze the security and resiliency of the smart grids. The distinct features included in this book are formal modeling of smart grid configurations, proactive and noninvasive verification of smart grid security and resiliency properties, identification of potential threats, and corresponding mitigations. This book includes various illustrative case studies and extensive evaluation results demonstrating the efficacy of the formal techniques. We expect this book will maximize reader insights into theoretical and practical aspects of applying formal methods for the protection of critical infrastructures.

Charlotte, NC, USA   Ehab Al-Shaer
Cookeville, TN, USA   Mohammad Ashiqur Rahman
February 2016

Acknowledgements

Special thanks to Dr. Rajesh Kavasseri (North Dakota State University, USA), Dr. Rakesh Bobba (Oregon State University, USA), Dr. Padmalochan Bera (IIT Bhubaneswar, India), and Muhammad Qasim Ali (Goldman Sachs, USA) for their precious inputs to this text.

We also want to thank Susan Lagerstrom-Fife, Editor, Computer Science, Springer, USA for her support and advice on this book. We would also like to thank Jennifer Malat, Assistant Editor, Computer science, Springer, USA for her efforts.

Contents

Acronyms

A list of selected acronyms that are often used in this book:

AGC	Automatic Generation Control
AMI	Advanced Metering Infrastructure
AMR	Automatic Meter Reading
CPS	Cyber-Physical System
CTL	Computation Tree Logic
DC	Direct Current
DDoS	Distributed Denial of Service
D-FACTS	Distributed Flexible AC Transmission System
DTMC	Discrete-Time Markov Chain
EMS	Energy Management System
FERC	Federal Energy Regulatory Commission
GPS	Global Positioning System
HAN	Home Area Network
HMI	Human Machine Interface
ICS	Industrial Control System
IDS	Intrusion Detection System
IED	Intelligent Electronic Device
IPSec	Internet Protocol Security
LMC	Labeled Markov Chain
LTL	Linear Temporal Logic
MDP	Markov Decision Process
MTD	Moving Target Defense
MTU	Master Terminal Unit
NAN	Neighborhood Area Network
NERC	North American Electric Reliability Corporation
NIST	National Institute of Standards and Technology
NMS	Network Management System
OPF	Optimal Power Flow
PDC	Phasor Data Concentrator

PLC	Programmable Logic Controller
PMU	Phasor Measurement Unit
ROC	Receiver Operating Characteristics
RTU	Remote Terminal Unit
SAT	Boolean Satisfiability Problem
SCADA	Supervisory Control and Data Acquisition
SMT	Satisfiability Modulo Theories
TPM	Trusted Platform Module
UFDI	Undetected False Data Injection
WAN	Wide Area Network

Part I
Introduction

This part includes discussions on various background topics with regards to smart grid security and resiliency. First chapter presents preliminaries about smart grid core components and corresponding security challenges. The second chapter briefly talks about formal methods and model checking. The last chapter summarizes the formal models presented in this book.

Chapter 1
Smart Grids and Security Challenges

Smart grids are the modernization of the legacy power systems with the development of communication infrastructures. They are perfect examples of cyber-physical systems (CPS). To delineate the importance of the safety and reliability of smart grids, the Schneider Electric report in June 2010 can be cited [4]: "The financial impact of power disruption was demonstrated during the August 2003 blackout, which affected 45 million people in eight US states and 10 million people in parts of Canada. Healthcare facilities experienced hundreds of millions of dollars in lost revenue from canceled services, legal liability, and damaged reputations. Six hospitals were in bankruptcy one year later." This incident clearly illustrates the extent of the impact due to operational interruption in energy networks.

Since communication infrastructures are integrated with the legacy systems, a smart grid exhibits a hybrid configuration comprised of heterogeneous cyber-physical components. This integration leads to various vulnerabilities and potential security threats. An execution of such a threat can easily cause devastating damages to the grid. Therefore, there is a great need for security analytics to (1) verify the compliance of smart grid configurations with security standards (provided by NIST, NERC, and FERC [3, 5, 6]), (2) identify potential threats on smart grids, and (3) design necessary defense mechanisms. This need for smart grid security can be reflected by the following major security challenges:

1. Proactive identification of potential security threats and remediation plan synthesis for their mitigation,
2. Dynamic security design that make the behavior unpredictable for the attacker while keeping it deterministic for the system.
3. Automated security analytics that offer efficient verification and synthesis of smart grid security properties.

This book presents a list of solutions that address these challenges. This chapter provides a brief overview of a smart grid, the potential attacks on it, and corresponding security goals and challenges.

© Springer International Publishing Switzerland 2016
E. Al-Shaer, M.A. Rahman, *Security and Resiliency Analytics for Smart Grids*,
Advances in Information Security 67, DOI 10.1007/978-3-319-32871-3_1

1.1 Smart Grid Overview

In the last decade, the paradigm of power grid infrastructures has been shifted to a new age. Legacy infrastructures are being replaced with state-of-the-art smart grids. Leading utility providers in the U.S. have taken different initiatives for deploying smart devices by replacing the existing legacy systems [8]. Smart grids provide intelligent devices with two-way communications among them, which allow efficient management of the power while providing useful features. The basic reason for moving to smart grids is to provide uninterrupted low-cost energy considering twenty-first century demands. However, a smart grid exhibits a hybrid infrastructure as it usually consist of numerous cyber and physical smart devices along with legacy equipment, wherein a device often needs to communicate with other devices. Smart grids are designated as critical infrastructures. Thus, they require very rigid security considerations.

Figure 1.1 presents a basic conceptual architecture of a smart grid. It shows different components of smart grids and their inter-connections. A detailed diagram of a smart grid is presented in Fig. 1.2, which shows the power generation, transmission, and distribution. The figure also illustrates the major measuring and controlling systems of the grid, including the communication infrastructures and the control and utility centers.

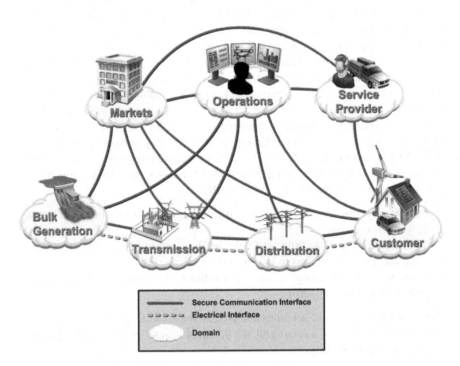

Fig. 1.1 A conceptual model of the smart grid architecture [5]

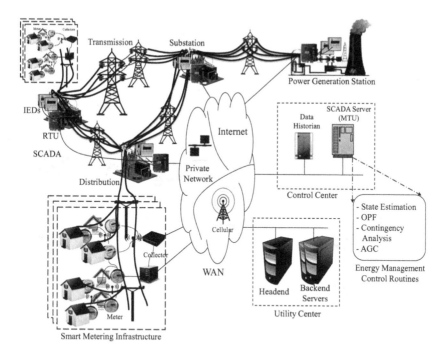

Fig. 1.2 A detailed architecture of a smart grid, which shows the end-to-end power transmission and distribution, AMI and SCADA communication infrastructures, and the utility and control centers

1.2 AMI

Advanced metering infrastructure (AMI) is one of the core components of a smart grid. This system measures, collects, and analyzes energy usage by the electricity customers. A typical AMI consists of a large number of smart meters and intelligent data collectors. Data collectors communicate with smart meters either on request or on a schedule, collect data, and send the report to the utility center through a backhaul communication system. In fact, AMI is an extended version of the existing automatic meter reading (AMR) technology by the addition of two-way communication capability, allowing commands to be sent toward the meters for different purposes like demand-response actions or remote service disconnects [7, 9]. The utility center is mainly responsible for billing the energy users for their usage. The scope of the utility center is broadening with the implementation of AMI. Different demand-response utility services are being established in order to efficiently manage the electricity usage by reducing the energy cost as well as the energy loss or theft.

A typical topology of the AMI network can be found in Fig. 1.2, which is elaborated in Fig. 1.3. Usually a meter establishes an authenticated connection with a specific collector to report energy usage data. A collector forwards this data to the utility center over a trusted path. The server at the utility center that receives this

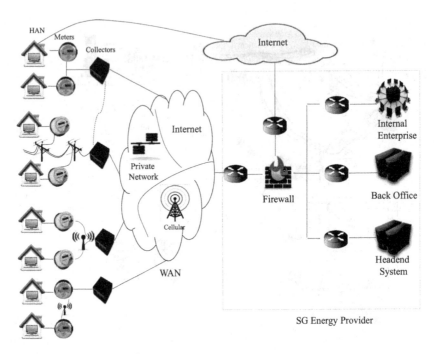

Fig. 1.3 A typical AMI topology

data is often named as the headend system. The control commands from the headend to the meters are also transmitted through secure connections. A meter is connected to a collector directly or through another meter. In the latter case, geographically co-located meters form a mesh network. Heterogeneous communication links or communication systems are seen in AMI. For example, communication medium can be power-line, wi-fi, ethernet, or optical fiber, communication mode can be cellular or serial, and communication infrastructures can be proprietary or third-party. The collectors are usually connected with the utility center through a wide area network (WAN).

There are two data delivery modes, which can be used between a meter and a collector, and between a collector and a headend system: (1) push-driven mode (simply, push mode) in which a meter or a collector reports data periodically based on a pre-configured delivery schedule, and (2) pull-driven mode (simply, pull mode) in which a meter or a collector reports data only upon receiving a request. In the pull mode, requests are usually sent periodically following a schedule. In practice, the push mode is used between a meter and a collector, while the pull mode is used between a collector and the headend system, as shown in Fig. 1.4.

There is also a provision to allow an energy user's home area network (HAN) to be connected with the AMI network through the smart meters. There are also different proprietary communication protocols used in AMI other than TCP/IP.

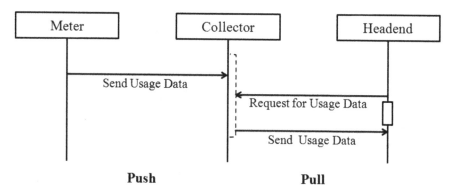

Fig. 1.4 The push and pull modes of data delivery in smart grids

LonTalk is an example of such protocols which is often used between a meter and a collector. An AMI network also involves varieties of data stream types like energy usage data, control commands, and software patches.

1.3 SCADA

In the energy transmission and distribution side of the smart grid, different communication networks exist for sensing measurements and transmitting control commands. These networks are associated with the supervisory control and data acquisition (SCADA) system. SCADA is the major industrial control system (ICS) in smart grids, and connects the generating stations, substations, and control centers. SCADA is mainly responsible for monitoring and controlling the remote equipment by obtaining data from the remote devices, analyzing the received data at the control centers, and executing necessary control commands at the remote devices. It can be noticed in Figs. 1.1 and 1.5 that the control centers associated with the generation, transmission, and distribution systems are connected to the physical power system using cyber infrastructure.

Figure 1.5 represents a typical SCADA topology in detail. There are various kinds of SCADA devices, such as SCADA servers or master terminal units (MTUs), human machine interfaces (HMIs), data historians, and different field devices. Remote terminal units (RTUs), programmable logic controllers (PLCs), and intelligent electronic devices (IEDs) are the typical field devices. IEDs often receive data from sensors, while they actuate the control commands received from the SCADA control server. IEDs and PLCs are also designed to take pre-specified actions automatically when the designated situations occur. RTUs are mainly data collecting and forwarding devices. Similar to AMI, there are different communication links in SCADA. The modem-based serial communication is often seen in SCADA for the communication between RTUs and MTUs. The SCADA communication is done

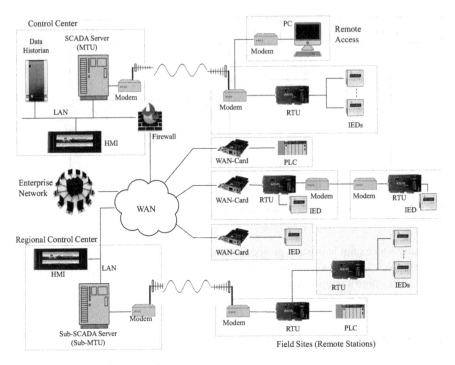

Fig. 1.5 A typical SCADA topology

using industrial protocols like Modbus, DNP3, or IEC 61850, which are layered protocol similar to TCP/IP. Some variants of these protocols are built on top of the TCP/IP communication architecture.

In addition to legacy SCADA devices, smart grids are currently being equipped with phasor measurement units (PMUs), also known as synchrophasors, which are capable of measuring both voltage and current phasor measurements with a precisely synchronized timestamp. PMUs are often connected with a global positioning system (GPS), which allows them to be synchronized with microsecond accuracy. There are phasor data concentrators (PDCs) that collect the phasor measurements from connected PMUs, sort the measurements according to the GPS timestamp, and provide this data to the control server.

The control server takes the sensor measurements from field devices through the power network and sends the control commands to them after analyzing the data using the same infrastructure. There are different control modules or routines to manage the grid efficiently and reliably. These modules are specified together as the energy management system (EMS). As Figs. 1.2 and 1.6 illustrate, EMS includes state estimation, optimal power flow (OPF), contingency analysis, and automatic generation control (AGC) as its main control modules. These modules are interdependent with each other, and one's outputs are often used as inputs for others. The state estimation is the core component of EMS. Its function is to compute

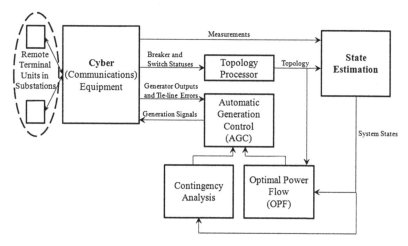

Fig. 1.6 A simpler schematic diagram of the energy management system

the unknown state variables of the power system from the sensor measurements received through the SCADA system. The output of state estimation is used in OPF and contingency analysis. The objective of the OPF process is to minimize the total generation cost satisfying the load and the operating constraints (e.g., capacities of the transmission lines). Contingency analysis is important for maintaining the system's security in contingencies, such as generation unit failures and transmission line breakages. Outputs of these modules are finally used by AGC, which adjusts the power outputs of generators at different power plants such that the grid operates optimally with respect to the generation cost and the physical safety of the grid.

1.4 Potential Threats

Communication infrastructures are integrated with the legacy systems in a smart grid, which produce a hybrid configuration comprised of heterogeneous cyber-physical components. Moreover, these cyber-physical components are often inter-connected through different communication media and protocols, and they are operated in different modes and policies. The inherent complexity of integrating multiple heterogeneous systems in a smart grid significantly increases the potential of security threats, which can cause massive and extremely devastating damage. It is well documented that configuration errors cause 50–80 % of vulnerabilities in cyber infrastructures [1]. Since smart grids are still evolving, weak security measures often exist there. In fact, it is possible that there is no security measure present at all. As a result, cyber attacks can happen easily. The causes and impacts of potential threats to smart grids categorized into the following types:

Attacks on Connectivity In order to send or receive necessary measurements, commands, etc., communication must be established between the sender and the receiver. In AMI, there should be a path between the smart meters and the utility servers, so that billing reports can reach the utility from the meters, while control commands (e.g., meter turn on or off) from the utility can reach the designated meters. There are typically intermediate devices for collecting, buffering, and forwarding the data between the meters and the utility. In SCADA, power flow measurements must reach the control centers, often through the intermediate devices, so that state estimation and control routines can be performed. However, a connectivity requirement may fail due to misconfigured devices, link failures, or compromised intermediate nodes.

Attacks on Data Integrity Data integrity is crucial for the smart grid operations. If data (e.g., measurements or control commands) is corrupted, then corresponding applications may fail and serious cascading effects may occur. Due to the lack of data integrity protection, cyber attacks like man-in-the-middle and replay attacks can be launched, and the data can be maliciously modified. In AMI, such false data injection attacks can create incorrect billing, broken service, and inaccurate demand-response [2]. In the case of a SCADA system, incorrect state estimation can cause inefficient or incorrect control decisions that may create serious economical as well as physical damage to the grid. For example, with the corrupted states, the OPF process will generate a non-optimal solution for power generation outputs. This solution may be not only economically expensive but also physically damaging, as it can lead electricity to flow through some transmission lines higher than their critical limits. Similarly, the contingency analysis with corrupted states will have an erroneous perception of security in contingencies.

Attacks on Data or Service Availability Smart grids are also subject to denial of service (DoS), link flooding, and wireless link jamming attacks. For example, in the case of a RF mesh network-based smart metering infrastructure, the communication between smart meters and the associated collector can be disrupted by creating radio jamming. More interestingly, incorrect scheduling of usage data reports can also lead to self-generated DoS attacks because it may cause overflowing of a data collector's buffer. DoS attacks can cause data to be lost or delayed in reaching the destination, which consequently can make different utility services fail due to inadequate or out-of-date data. For example, if state estimation is done using delayed data, the computed states can be too old to make a correct control decision.

1.5 Security Goals and Challenges

The correct operation of a smart grid requires consistent and secure data flow and the timely execution of tasks. In order to ensure safe, secure, and reliable functioning of smart grids, our objective in this dissertation is to presents solutions for different major security issues:

1.5.1   Security Goals

In order to make the smart grid system secure and dependable, the following three goals are required to achieve:

Proactive Analysis for Security and Resiliency Reactive security using intrusion response and mitigation is insufficient for critical CPS like smart grids. Unlike traditional IT systems, where the impact of an attack is mostly local, an attack in a critical infrastructure can be devastating in terms of damages and consequences. Thus, it is required to proactively identify the potential threats in order to reduce the attack surface for a smart grid and avoid the detrimental consequences.

Dynamic Measures for Security and Resiliency This is the ability to provide security and resiliency to smart grids by introducing agility to the system properties so that the potential knowledge of the adversary about the target reduces and thus the capability of launching attack minimizes. With the growing nature of the attack surface, critical infrastructures like smart grids should be resilient to zero day attacks. Dynamic security measures increase the resiliency of the system against unknown vulnerabilities.

Automation in Analysis Automating the security analysis is essential for large and hybrid systems like smart grids, as manual security analysis is quite unrealistic. The smart grid security guidelines developed by NIST [5] are highly detailed and cumbersome to implement due to the complexity of cyber and physical integrations. Therefore, automating security verification and configuration synthesis techniques in a provable and scalable manner is a"holy-grail" challenge for the dependability of smart grids.

1.5.2   Challenges

Toward solving the security goals for a system that integrates cyber and physical components like a smart grid, there are many challenges that must be addressed. The key challenges are as follows:

- Integration of cyber and physical systems: Since cyber and physical systems are included together in AMI and SCADA, along with the coexistence of smart devices with legacy systems, modeling this integration is challenging.
- Interdependency modeling: There often exist various interdependencies among different components in AMI and SCADA. For example, the output from the state estimation process is taken as an input to the OPF process. Thus, it is crucial to investigate such interdependencies and model them accordingly in order to understand the broader space of attack and impact.

- Evasion modeling: There are algorithms to detect bad measurements in SCADA. However, it is possible to corrupt the data without being detected by evading these algorithms. It is important to inspect existing as well as potential evasion techniques, and find defense mechanisms for them.
- Security and resiliency property modeling: There are security guidelines for AMI and SCADA provided by NIST. It is quite challenging to translate these guidelines into logical constraints, considering different AMI and SCADA components and their interactions.
- Generic property modeling: Various energy providers may have different security requirements. Thus, it is important to provide a general framework that allows defining new requirements or constraints with minimum or no change to the existing model.
- Scalability: A smart grid usually consists of a large number of field devices. For example, an AMI typically consists of thousands of smart meters and hundreds of data collectors. It is challenging to model this large number of devices such that the security verification, as well as the resiliency architecture synthesis, can be performed efficiently.

1.6   Summary

This chapter presents a brief overview of smart grids, particularly AMI and SCADA topology, cyber and physical devices, communications, and security configurations. The potential attacks on smart grids are discussed in short, followed by the security goals and corresponding challenges to be addressed. The following chapter discusses the idea of formal analysis, an effective technical approach, to solve the smart grid security goals. The corresponding formal analytics are elaborated in the second part of this book.

References

1. R. Alimi, Y. Wang, Y.R. Yang, Shadow configuration as a network management primitive, in *ACM SIGCOMM Conference on Data Communication* (2008), pp. 111–122
2. Energy Research Council, Best practices: demand response (2013), http://energyresearchcouncil.com/downloads/ERCResearchBriefDemandResponse.pdf
3. Federal Energy Regulatory Commission (2015), http://www.ferc.gov/, http://www.ferc.gov/industries/electric/indus-act/reliability/standards.asp. Accessed 2015
4. B. Lawrence, M. Hancock, G. Stieva, How unreliable power affects the business value of a hospital. Schneider Electr. (2010), http://www.schneider-electric.com/documents/support/white-papers/wp_healthcare-how-unreliable-power.pdf
5. National Institute of Standards and Technology (2015), U.S. Department of Commerce, http://www.nist.gov/, http://www.nist.gov/publication-portal. Accessed 2015
6. North American Electric Reliability Corporation (2015), http://www.nerc.com, http://www.nerc.com/pa/Stand/Pages/default.aspx. Accessed 2015

7. Silver Spring, How the smart grid makes restoration faster and easier for utilities (2012), http://www.silverspringnet.com/wp-content/uploads/SilverSpring-ExecutiveSummary-Outage.pdf
8. The Smart Grid: An Introduction, U.S. Department of Energy (2008), http://energy.gov/oe/downloads/smart-grid-introduction-0
9. J.S. Vardakas, N. Zorba, C.V. Verikoukis, A survey on demand response programs in smart grids: pricing methods and optimization algorithms, in *IEEE Communications Surveys Tutorials* (2014), pp. 1–1

Chapter 2
Analytics for Smart Grid Security and Resiliency

The security and resiliency analysis of a smart grid needs to consider the target component(s), flexible attack model, and the integration among different smart grid components and attack properties. An exhaustive security analysis is not only expensive but also infeasible using testbeds. Formal analytics can play an important role toward comprehensive security analysis of the system, which can identify potential threats provably, that can further be verified on testbeds.

Recent research studies have established the capability of formal models for analyzing security and resiliency of different components of a smart grid [1, 19, 21–25]. The proactive identification of security threats is performed by developing formal security verification techniques that discover cyber and physical security threats on different components of smart grids, including AMI, SCADA, and EMS. Dynamic security schemes for smart grids are designed with the idea of security by agility. In particular, these schemes make the behavior unpredictable for the attacker by frequently randomizing various critical parameters in the smart grid system, whilst keeping it deterministic for the system. These techniques provide automatic analysis of security properties and synthesis of threat mitigation plans ensuring the security and resiliency of the system. This chapter summarizes the formal analytics presented in this book and presents an overview of the technical approach. Finally, it briefly discusses about the tools used for formal modeling.

2.1 Formal Analytics

There are formal techniques and tools that can address the security requirements, identify potential threats, and offer remediation plans for smart grids, so that secure and reliable smart grids can be established. These techniques mostly focus on

© Springer International Publishing Switzerland 2016
E. Al-Shaer, M.A. Rahman, *Security and Resiliency Analytics for Smart Grids*,
Advances in Information Security 67, DOI 10.1007/978-3-319-32871-3_2

AMI, SCADA, and EMS, the most critical components of a smart grid (Fig. 1.2). The formal analytics for smart grid security and resiliency falls can be described in the following three major categories:

Security Analytics for AMI and SCADA A scalable and provable formal framework is presented that can verify the compliance of AMI configurations with NIST security guidelines [15], and generate remediation plans for potential security violations. This framework is implemented as a tool named SmartAnalyzer, which enables energy providers to proactively investigate AMI security configurations in order to identify and mitigate potential security threats and to guarantee AMI operational integrity and security requirements. The uniqueness of this framework lies in the formal modeling of novel security properties that are critical for the integrity and security of AMI. These security properties include different invariant and user-driven constraints, such as data overflow/overwrite protection, cyber bandwidth limitation, data integrity and confidentiality, assured report delivery, and data freshness. An identical formal model for the proactive security analysis of SCADA is also presented. This model focuses on verifying the integrity of the SCADA control routines along with the trusted communication between field devices and the control center.

Security Analytics for EMS Modules A formal model is illustrated that can verify stealthy false data injection attacks against state estimation, a core control module in EMS. This framework models potential attack evasions on state estimation, interdependency between state estimation, and other EMS modules, and a comprehensive list of attack attributes, such as access capability, resource constraint, knowledge limitation, and attack goal. A solution to this model provides the attack vectors (e.g., the set of measurements to be altered) required for compromising state estimation. More importantly, the modeling of interdependent modules together allows one to investigate novel stealthy attacks on state estimation. A mechanism is also presented, based on this attack verification framework, that can systematically design a security architecture for state estimation, which includes a minimal set of measurements (or associated buses) that requires data integrity protection. In addition, a dynamic defense mechanism is demonstrated that can defend persistent attacks to some extent by randomizing different critical parameters used in state estimation.

Intrusion Detection Systems for AMI Unlike traditional networks, smart grid has its own unique challenges, such as limited computational power devices and potentially high deployment cost, that restrict the deployment options of intrusion detectors. Experiments results are presented showing that a smart grid exhibits deterministic and predictable behavior that can be accurately modeled to detect intrusion. However, this deterministic behavior can also be leveraged by an attacker to launch evasive attacks. In this respect, a robust mutation based intrusion detection system (IDS) is presented that makes the behavior unpredictable for the attacker whilst keeping it deterministic for the system. The AMI behavior is modeled using event logs collected at intelligent data collectors, which in turn can be verified using the specifications invariant generated from the AMI behavior and mutable configuration. Event logs are modeled using fourth order Markov Chain and specifications are written in linear temporal logic (LTL). A configuration randomization module is presented that counters evasion and mimicry attacks. The approach provides robustness against evasion and mimicry attacks to a certain extent.

2.2 Technical Approach Overview

The technical approach applied in developing the formal models for smart grid security and resiliency analysis exhibits the following major features:

1. Formally modeling smart grid components and corresponding security and resiliency verification and synthesis problems
2. Encoding the formal models using formal languages, in particular satisfiability modulo theories (SMT) and linear temporal logics
3. Solving the encoded or implemented formal models using suitable SMT or model checking solvers
4. Evaluating the solutions in order to conduct performance analysis and scalability assessment

These technical features are briefly discussed below with respect to formal analytics presented in this book.

2.2.1 Security Analytics for AMI and SCADA

The correct functioning of the smart grid system depends on the security configurations of the smart grid devices and the secure interactions among them across the network. NIST has developed security guidelines, especially NISTIR 7628 and NIST SP 800-82 for AMI and SCADA security [9, 15, 27]. NERC also provides cyber security requirements for bulk electric power systems [16, 17]. These guidelines consist of numerous security controls that ensure secure and trusted communication and resource availability toward controlling potential security threats on AMI and SCADA. There is a large number of logical relations among the configuration parameters of AMI and SCADA devices, that must be satisfied in order to comply with these guidelines and ensure the integrity and security of smart grid operations. A formal framework can verify smart grid security configurations with standard and organizational security guidelines and identify potential security threats as violations of those security requirements [19, 21]. The major technical novelty of this framework is its capability to analyze various operational integrity and security constraints on AMI and SCADA, which are often different than those used in conventional IT systems. The security analysis is conducted based on an SMT-based formal mechanism.

In the case of AMI security analysis, the framework formally models the AMI topology and device configurations and the corresponding security requirements according to NISTIR 7628. A property-based abstraction is applied to model the configurations of AMI devices, so that the model can scale efficiently with the thousands of smart meters and hundreds of data collectors. The model is solved using an efficient SMT solver, Z3 [30], which verifies whether the asserted clauses (i.e., constraints) within the model satisfy each other. A violation of the constraint satisfaction indicates a threat. When there is a constraint violation, the solver's outcome is systematically analyzed to identify the potential causes of the threat. This diagnosis mechanism also identifies remediation strategies to mitigate this threat. The identified threats and remediation plans are presented to smart grid operators to fix the security breaches. Its scalability is also evaluated with the help of synthetic AMI networks in terms of time and memory requirements.

In the case of SCADA security analysis, the security requirements should consider NIST SP 800-82 security guidelines, although there is a strong similarity between the security guidelines of NISTIR 7628 and NIST SP 800-82. Therefore, this book presents a formal analysis that principally focuses on security and resiliency requirements specific to SCADA [26]. The secure data communication from the field devices to the control center is required for the secure operation of SCADA control routines with trusted data. The objective of this analysis is to verify the resiliency of performing the control routines in contingencies, i.e., potential threats when some field devices are unavailable due to cyber attacks or accidental failures.

2.2.2   Security Analytics for EMS Modules

The formal framework presented for the security analysis of EMS modules, particularly state estimation, characterizes attacks in their most general form so that adversarial capabilities against the power system can be modeled [20]. An attack is modeled in terms of different attributes including the adversary's accessibility, resources, and knowledge. The attack feasibility is assessed by considering these attributes simultaneously. The dynamics of state estimation with respect to the measurements, adversary attributes, and attack evasion properties are formally modeled using SMT logics. The solution to this model answers whether an attack can be launched stealthily in a particular attack scenario. Thus, this formal framework allows for the exploration of potential threats under different attack scenarios.

This framework allows for modeling the interdependency among different EMS modules, which broadens the security analysis capability. The modeling of topology poisoning attacks with regards to the topology processor explores novel stealthy attacks on state estimation [23]. The modeling of OPF verifies the impact of stealthy attacks on the economic operation of the grid as well as its stability [22, 24]. An automated mechanism is devised based on this security analysis results that systematically synthesizes a set of measurements (or buses) that need to be secured, in order to make state estimation immune from stealthy bad data injection while considering the grid operator's resources and assumed attack model.

A novel idea of introducing dynamic behavior in the system is offered to provide a proactive security to the grid [25]. This moving target defense (MTD) based mechanism randomizes the physical parameters that are related to the state estimation process. This technique employs frequent and operationally safe randomization of (1) the set of measurements used for state estimation and (2) the electrical properties, particularly impedance, of a set of power transmission lines. Due to the frequent randomization of these properties, an adversary cannot gain the perfect knowledge required to successfully launch a stealthy attack. As a result, the attack success probability reduces significantly. This mechanism includes two formal models in order to select valid randomization considering different operating constraints of the grid, such as (1) ensuring the observability of the power system from the received measurements and (2) maintaining the existing optimal power flow solution. The scalability of this formal framework is evaluated using standard IEEE test power systems along with synthetic attack scenarios.

2.2.3 Intrusion Detection Systems for AMI

The deployment of a detection module at the data collector provides the benefit of monitoring both the meter-collector and the collector-headend communications. The logs collected at the collectors can be exploited for monitoring and characterizing the AMI behavior. Since AMI is a special purpose network, its traffic dynamics are often low. These AMI features need to be considered while developing an IDS for AMI. AMI behavior is deterministic which allows an attacker to evade intrusion detection systems by imitating the behavior. To make it robust against evasion, a model checking-based IDS can mutate the AMI behavior [1]. In this technique, the behavior is kept deterministic for the collector by using a pre-shared secret key.

The AMI infrastructure behavior is modeled using the logs generated at the smart collector. Since stochastic model based on fourth order Markov chain exhibits a low conditional entropy, it is used to represent the AMI probabilistic behavior, which depends on the configuration and nature of the AMI network. Behavior specifications are automatically generated from the a-priori known configurations of the AMI devices. These specifications are expressed in LTL and probabilistically verified using the stochastic model generated from the smart collector's logs using PRISM model checker [18]. Experimentations are performed on a real-world dataset which evaluate the efficacy of this technique.

2.3   Overview of SMT and Probabilistic Model Checking

This section briefly introduces SMT and probabilistic model checking, which are the building-blocks of the formal analytics presented in this book.

2.3.1   Satisfiability Modulo Theories

In the past decade, Boolean formal methods (e.g., SAT [13, 14]) have been used successfully in network security analysis, especially for verifying security policy, which is defined as a sequence of propositional logical constraints [2, 4]. However, due to the increasing complexity of network security and business requirements of CPS, Boolean propositional logic constraints are not suitable to develop security analytics for complex systems like smart grids. SMT overcomes this shortcoming. SMT offers various "background theories" that efficiently deal with integers, real numbers, arrays, uninterpreted functions, linear arithmetic, etc. In addition, SMT solvers provide a much richer formal modeling platform compared to SAT solvers.

SMT solvers are proved to be powerful tools in solving constraint satisfaction problems that arise in many diverse areas including software and hardware verification, type inference, extended static checking, test-case generation, scheduling, planning, graph problems, etc. [5, 7]. An SMT instance is a formula in first-order logic, where some functions and predicate symbols have additional interpretations according to the background theories. SMT is the problem of determining whether a formula is satisfiable or not. For example, the following simple SMT instance has two constraints:

$$(2x + y < 2) \vee (x - 2y > 0)$$

$$x \leq 1$$

This instance is satisfied with the assignments: $x = 0$ and $y = 0$. There can be other assignments for x and y which can satisfy the constraints, and SMT can provide all of these assignments. SMT solvers are efficiently applied in solving large and complex problems. It has been shown that modern SMT solvers can check formulas with hundreds of thousands of variables, and millions of clauses [5, 7]. In this research, we primarily use theories of integers, real numbers, and linear arithmetic for modeling, and we find that our models are highly efficient in solving complex security problems in smart grids.

2.3.1.1   Z3

Z3 is a state-of-the art SMT solver being developed and maintained at Microsoft Research [30]. This solver can check the satisfiability of logical formulas over one or more theories. Z3 supports different theories, such as arithmetic, fixed-size bit-vectors, extensional arrays, datatypes, uninterpreted functions, and quantifiers. Although the core language of Z3 is SMT-LIB 2.0, it provides useful APIs for high-level languages, namely C, C++, C#, Java, and Python, for flexible encoding. There is an online interface to try Z3 in SMT-LIB [29]. In the following, a toy example is presented to illustrate the idea of solving a problem using Z3.

Example. A Novish network security administrator needs to design a security architecture for the network. Before starting this complex job, he wants to rank different types of security devices according to the partially known security enforcing capabilities. There are five kinds of security devices to be ordered, namely firewall, IPSec, IDS, proxy, and network address translation (NAT). The administrator needs to rank these device types according to the available partial orders as follows:

   i. Firewall performs better than IPSec.
  ii. Proxy performs no better than NAT.
 iii. IDS performs better than NAT, but less than IPSec.

If F, I, D, N, and P are ranks of firewall, IPSec, IDS, NAT, and proxy, respectively, the partial orders can be represented formally as follows:

$$F > I$$

$$P \leq N$$

$$(D > N) \wedge (D < I)$$

As there are five kinds of devices, the ranks will be 1 and 5. That is:

$$(F \geq 1) \wedge (F \leq 5)$$

The same is true for the other variables. Table 2.1 shows the corresponding SMT-LIB encoding (column 1) and the Z3 solver's output (column 2). Two satisfiable solutions are shown in the table. The second solution is received when the first satisfiable result is taken out from the search space by adding its negation as an constraint. It is worth mentioning that there are four more alternative satisfiable results.

2.3.2   Probabilistic Model Checking

Model checking is an automatic formal verification technique for finite state concurrent systems [6]. The system is represented using a finite-state model and the system requirements are specified using propositional temporal logic. A model checker verifies the formal design if all the specifications are satisfied. When the result is false, the model checker produces a counterexample that can be investigated to pinpoint the source of the error. LTL and computational tree logic (CTL) are popular languages for specifying requirements for model checking.

Table 2.1 An example of SMT-LIB encoding and corresponding output

; Declarations
(declare-const F Int)
(declare-const I Int)
(declare-const D Int)
(declare-const P Int)
(declare-const N Int)
 	
; Constraints
; Partial Orders
(assert (> F I))
(assert (<= P N))
(assert (and (> D N) (< D I)))
 	
; Order should within a limit
(assert (and (> F 0) (<= F 5)))
(assert (and (> I 0) (<= I 5)))
(assert (and (> D 0) (<= D 5)))
(assert (and (> P 0) (<= P 5)))
(assert (and (> N 0) (<= N 5)))
 	
(check-sat)
(get-model) ; Output 1
 	
; To get the next satisfiable solution
(assert (not (and (= N 1) (= P 1)
          (= D 2) (= I 3) (= F 4))))
 	
(check-sat)
(get-model) ; Output 2
	; Output 1
	sat
	(model
	  (define-fun N () Int
	    1)
	  (define-fun P () Int
	    1)
	  (define-fun D () Int
	    2)
	  (define-fun F () Int
	    4)
	  (define-fun I () Int
	    3)
	)
	
	; Output 2
	sat
	(model
	  (define-fun N () Int
	    1)
	  (define-fun P () Int
	    1)
	  (define-fun D () Int
	    2)
	  (define-fun F () Int
	    5)
	  (define-fun I () Int
	    3)
	)

Probabilistic model checking is a formal verification technique for modeling and analyzing systems that exhibit probabilistic behavior [12]. There are different kinds of probabilistic models. Popular model types are discrete-time Markov chain (DTMC), continuous-time Markov chain (CTMC), and Markov decision processes (MDP). System requirements are specified using probabilistic temporal logic (e.g., LTL and probabilistic CTL or PCTL). The output of model checking can be quantitative outcomes other than satisfiable and unsatisfiable results only.

Linear Temporal Logic LTL is an infinite sequence of states where each point in time has a unique successor according to a linear-time perspective [3]. LTL is sometimes called propositional temporal logic (PTL). Linear temporal property is a temporal logic formula that describes a set of infinite sequences for which a property is true. In model checking, a desired temporal property is specified using LTL operators and checked for its satisfaction with the model.

LTL is written up from a finite set of propositional variables (an alphabet), a set of basic logical operators, and a set of basic temporal operators. The set of LTL formulas over an alphabet Σ is inductively defined as follows:

$$\varphi ::= true \mid \sigma \mid \varphi_1 \wedge \varphi_2 \mid \neg\varphi \mid \bigcirc \varphi \mid \varphi_1 \cup \varphi_2$$

Here, $\sigma \in \Sigma$, $\neg$ (negation), and $\wedge$ (conjunction) are logical operators, and $\bigcirc$ (next) and $\cup$ (until) are temporal operators. Other than these fundamental operators there are additional operators in LTL formulas. For example, $\vee$ (disjunction), $\rightarrow$ (implication), and $\leftrightarrow$ (equivalence) are additional logical operators, while $\square$ (always or globally) and $\diamond$ (eventually or finally) are additional temporal operators. The temporal modalities can be combined together for further modalities, such as $\square\diamond$ (infinitely often) and $\diamond\square$ (eventually forever).

The temporal meaning of the above mentioned LTL operators are specified for further understanding:

- $\bigcirc$ (or **X**): The property "**X** A" is true for a path if formula A is true in its next state.
- $\cup$ (or **U**): The property "A **U** B" is true for a path if formula B is true in some state of the path and formula A is true in all preceding states.
- $\diamond$ (or **F**): The property "**F** A" is true for a path if formula A eventually becomes true at some point along the path.
- $\square$ (or **G**): The property "**G** A" is true of a path if formula A remains true at all states along the path.

2.3.2.1 PRISM

PRISM is a popular probabilistic model checker [11, 12]. This tool has been successfully used to analyze systems that exhibit random or probabilistic behavior, such as communication and multimedia protocols, randomized distributed algorithms, security protocols, biological systems, and many others. PRISM supports different probabilistic models including DTMCs, CTMCs, and MDPs. PRISM offers a simple, state-based language to describe models. It also provides support for automated analysis of numerous quantitative properties of a model. Example queries can be like "Is the probability of a failure that can cause one-third of the system down more than 25 %?", "what is the worst-case probability of the protocol terminating in error in a given initial scenario?", or "what can be the maximum number of messages that may be needed for a set of distributed nodes to reach a consensus based on a protocol?". The property specification language supports different temporal logics including LTL, PCTL, and probabilistic soft logic (PSL). PRISM is free and open source and it is released under the GNU general public license (GPL) [18]. A toy example of probabilistic model checking in PRISM is presented below [28].

Example. Figure 2.1 presents an example DTMC that implements the Knuth-Yao's probabilistic algorithm for obtaining a fair 6-sided die with a fair coin [8, 10]. As the graph shows, at every step (starting from state 0) a coin is tossed and there is 50 % chance of taking each of the two possible choices. The algorithm terminates when state 7 is reached at which one of the values (on the right-hand side) for the die is received. The objective of model checking is to verify the following two properties:

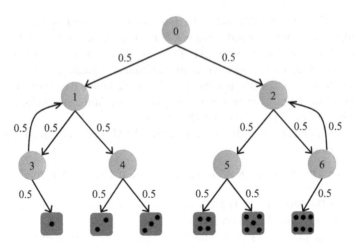

Fig. 2.1 A DTMC graph that implements the Knuth-Yao's probabilistic algorithm that emulates a "fair die"

- The probability, from the initial state of the model, of reaching a state where the die value is 2 or 3 is less than or equal to 50 %.
- With the probability greater than 10 %, state 5 of the model is eventually reached, followed immediately to a state at which the die value is equal or higher than 4.

The first property can be specified in LTL as follows: P < 0.5 [F s = 7 & (d = 2 | d=3)]. PRISM returns true for this property. It returns the corresponding probability value if P is unspecified as "P=?" in the LTL property specification. This probability is returned as 33 %. The LTL specification of LTL of the second property is P>0.2 [F (s=5 & (X (s=7 & d>=5)))]. PRISM returns false for this property. If P is unspecified as "P=?", the actual probability value of satisfying this property is found and it is around 0.1667 (Table 2.2).

2.4 Summary

This chapter discusses the idea of formal analysis as an effective technical approach that can effectively analyze the smart grid security and resiliency. It briefly discuss on SMT and model checking, the two formal methods applied for this formal analysis. The corresponding tools, namely Z3 and PRISM, are introduced with small examples that demonstrate their applications in implementing formal models. The corresponding formal analytics are presented in detail in the following chapters of this book.

Table 2.2 The PRISM code that models the example algorithm

```
dtmc

module die

    // Local state
    s : [0..7] init 0;
    // Value of the die
    d : [0..6] init 0;

    [] s=0 -> 0.5 : (s'=1) + 0.5 : (s'=2);
    [] s=1 -> 0.5 : (s'=3) + 0.5 : (s'=4);
    [] s=2 -> 0.5 : (s'=5) + 0.5 : (s'=6);
    [] s=3 -> 0.5 : (s'=1) + 0.5 : (s'=7) & (d'=1);
    [] s=4 -> 0.5 : (s'=7) & (d'=2) + 0.5 : (s'=7) & (d'=3);
    [] s=5 -> 0.5 : (s'=7) & (d'=4) + 0.5 : (s'=7) & (d'=5);
    [] s=6 -> 0.5 : (s'=2) + 0.5 : (s'=7) & (d'=6);
    [] s=7 -> (s'=7);

endmodule
```

References

1. M.Q. Ali, E. Al-Shaer, Randomization-based intrusion detection system for advanced metering infrastructure*. ACM Trans. Inf. Syst. Secur. **18**(2), 1–30 (2015)
2. E. Al-Shaer et al., Network configuration in a box: towards end-to-end verification of network reachability and security, in *IEEE International Conference on Network Protocols (ICNP)*, NY (2009), pp. 107–116
3. C. Baier, J.P. Katoen, *Principles of Model Checking* (The MIT Press, Cambridge, 2008)
4. P. Bera, S. Ghosh, P. Dasgupta, Policy based security analysis in enterprise networks: a formal approach. IEEE Trans. Netw. Serv. Manage. **7**(4), 231–243 (2010)
5. N. Bjørner, L. Moura, Z3^{10}: applications, enablers, challenges and directions, in *International Workshop on Constraints in Formal Verification* (2009)
6. E.M. Clarke, O. Grumberg, D. Peled (eds.), *Model Checking* (MIT Press, Cambridge, 1999)
7. L. de Moura, N. Bjørner, Satisfiability modulo theories: an appetizer, in *Brazilian Symposium on Formal Methods* (2009)
8. A.D. Gordon et al., Probabilistic programming, in *the 36th International Conference on Software Engineering*, Hyderabad (2014), pp. 167–181
9. Guide to Industrial Control Systems (ICS) Security, NIST Special Publication 800-82 (Revision 1) (2013), http://dx.doi.org/10.6028/NIST.SP.800-82r1
10. D. Knuth, A. Yao, The complexity of nonuniform random number generation, in *Algorithms and Complexity: New Directions and Recent Results* (Academic Press, New York, 1976)
11. M. Kwiatkowska, Probabilistic model checking with PRISM: an overview (2015), http://qav.comlab.ox.ac.uk/papers/acmper_prismperf.pdf
12. M. Kwiatkowska, G. Norman, D. Parker, Stochastic model checking, in *the 7th International Conference on Formal Methods for Performance Evaluation*, Bertinoro (2007), pp. 220–270
13. M.W. Moskewicz et al., Chaff: engineering an efficient SAT solver, in *Annual ACM IEEE Design Automation Conference* (2001)
14. R. Nieuwenhuis, A. Oliveras, On SAT modulo theories and optimization problems, in *Theory and Applications of Satisfiability Testing (SAT)*. Lecture Notes in Computer Science, vol. 4121 (Springer, New York, 2006), pp. 156–169

15. NISTIR 7628: Guidelines for Smart Grid Cyber Security, Smart Grid Inter-Operability Panel-Cyber Security Working Group (2010), http://www.nist.gov/smartgrid/upload/nistir-7628_total.pdf
16. North American Electric Reliability Corporation, Comments of the North American Electric Reliability Corporation in Response to NIST Smart Grid Cyber Security Strategy and Requirements (Draft NISTIR 7628) (2009)
17. North-American Electric Reliability Corporation, Critical Infrastructure Protection (CIP) Standards (2015), http://www.nerc.com/pa/Stand/Pages/CIPStandards.aspx. Accessed 2015
18. Probabilistic Symbolic Model Checker, PRISM (2015), http://www.prismmodelchecker.org/. Accessed 2015
19. M.A. Rahman, E. Al-Shaer, P. Bera, SmartAnalyzer: a noninvasive security threat analyzer for AMI smart grid, in *31st IEEE International Conference on Computer Communications (INFOCOM)* (2012), pp. 2255–2263
20. M.A. Rahman, E. Al-Shaer, Md. Rahman, A formal model for verifying stealthy attacks on state estimation in power grids, in *IEEE International Conference on Smart Grid Communications*, October 2013
21. M.A. Rahman, E. Al-Shaer, P. Bera, A noninvasive threat analyzer for advanced metering infrastructure in smart grid. IEEE Trans. Smart Grid **4**(1), 273–287 (2013)
22. M.A. Rahman, E. Al-Shaer, R. Kavasseri, A formal model for verifying the impact of stealthy attacks on optimal power flow in power grids, in *ACM/IEEE International Conference on Cyber-Physical Systems (ICCPS)*, April 2014
23. M.A. Rahman, E. Al-Shaer, R. Kavasseri, Security threat analytics and countermeasure synthesis for state estimation in smart power grids, in *IEEE/IFIP International Conference on Dependable Systems and Networks (DSN)*, June 2014
24. M.A. Rahman, E. Al-Shaer, R. Kavasseri, Impact analysis of topology poisoning attacks on economic operation of the smart power grid, in *IEEE 34th International Conference on Distributed Computing Systems (ICDCS)*, June 2014, pp. 649–659
25. M.A. Rahman, E. Al-Shaer, R.B. Bobba, Moving target defense for hardening the security of the power system state estimation, in *The First ACM Workshop on Moving Target Defense (MTD)*, Scottsdale (2014), pp. 59–68
26. M.A. Rahman, A. Jakaria, E. Al-Shaer, Formal analysis for dependable supervisory control and data acquisition in smart grids, in *IEEE/IFIP International Conference on Dependable Systems and Networks (DSN)*, June 2016
27. Recommended Security Controls for Federal Information Systems and Organizations, NIST special publication 800-53 (Revision 4) (2013), http://dx.doi.org/10.6028/NIST.SP.800-53r4
28. The Die Example (2015), http://www.prismmodelchecker.org/tutorial/die.php. Accessed 2015
29. Z3 @ rise4fun from Microsoft, Microsoft research (2015), http://rise4fun.com/z3. Accessed 2015
30. The Z3 Theorem Prover, Microsoft research, https://github.com/Z3Prover/z3/wiki

Part II
Formal Analytics for Secure and Resilient Smart Grids

This part presents formal frameworks that can analyze the security and resiliency of smart grids as well as risk mitigation techniques. These techniques are of two kinds: static and dynamic. Various static analyses for security verification and defense plan synthesis are found in all three chapters of this part, while the dynamic analysis based security design is studied in the last two chapters.

Part II
Formal Analytics for Secure and Resilient
Smart Grids

Chapter 3
Security Analytics for AMI and SCADA

The correct functioning of a smart grid stands on consistent and secure execution of tasks in time. The safe security configuration depends not only on the local device parameters but also on the secure interactions and flows of these parameters across the network. There is a significant number of logical constraints on configuration parameters of many smart grid devices, which need to be satisfied to ensure safe and secure communications among smart grid components. NIST has developed security guidelines (e.g., NISTIR 7628 and NIST SP 800-82 [4, 10]) consisting of hundreds of security controls for ensuring trusted path, resource availability, boundary security protection, etc., toward controlling different security threats on smart grids. Implementing these security controls in a scalable manner is one of the major challenges for analyzing smart grid security and resiliency.

This chapter presents an automated security analysis framework for smart grid networks, particularly AMI and SCADA. This framework takes smart grid configurations and organizational security requirements as inputs, formally models configurations and various security constraints, and verifies the compliances of the configurations with the constraints using satisfaction checking. A comprehensive threat report is produced as an outcome of this verification that includes the traces and reasoning behind various constraint violations and potential reconfiguration plans. Case studies and evaluation results are presented to demonstrate the performance of the framework. This security verification allows energy providers to objectively assess and investigate smart grid security configurations to identify and mitigate potential security threats, and to enforce smart grid operational and organizational security requirements.

The major technical novelty of the framework lies in its capability of analyzing various operational integrity and security critical constraints in smart grids. This chapter describes this framework with respect to AMI and SCADA. In the case of AMI, this framework models the data overwrite protection, device scheduling and cyber bandwidth constraints, assured data delivery, and data freshness, which are crucial security controls specific to AMI. Apart from these, the framework is

© Springer International Publishing Switzerland 2016
E. Al-Shaer, M.A. Rahman, *Security and Resiliency Analytics for Smart Grids*,
Advances in Information Security 67, DOI 10.1007/978-3-319-32871-3_3

capable of verifying various basic security properties, such as trusted path, data integrity, confidentiality, etc. The second part of this chapter presents this security framework with respect to SCADA, which primarily models the trusted or secure data communication from the field devices, so that SCADA control routines can operate with required measurements and valid data. This analysis framework is developed on top of the SMT-based formal model solving engine and provides a proof-based threat report as the outcome, which can be comprehensively used for fixing the identified threats.

3.1 Overview of the Security Analysis Framework

The smart grid security analysis framework offers the following functionalities:

- Providing an extensible global model abstraction capable of representing millions of smart grid (e.g., smart meters in AMI) configurations.
- Modeling various constraints formally and encoding them into SMT logics.
- Verifying the satisfaction of the constraints with smart grid configurations using an SMT solver.
- Identifying security threats from the constraint violations and providing security hardening plans by analyzing the verification results.

The architecture of the framework is shown in Fig. 3.1. First, the Parser module parses given smart grid configurations. The input regarding smart grid configurations is given following a formatted input file (often a CSV file). It consists of the device configurations, topology, communication between the devices, etc. Then, the

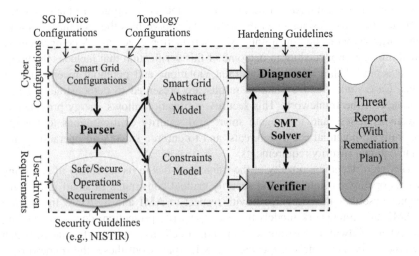

Fig. 3.1 The architecture of the security analysis framework

organizational requirements and various security guidelines are formally modeled as invariant and user-driven constraints, and these constraints are encoded into SMT logics with respect to the given smart grid configurations. Then, the Verifier module uses an SMT solver, particularly Z3 [3], to verify these constraints with the configurations. A comprehensive threat report is generated based on the verification results. These threats correspond to those constraints whose verifications are unsatisfied. Finally, the Hardener module creates a remediation plan by systematically analyzing the traces of unsatisfied results, which helps the administrators to reconfigure the corresponding smart grid system by directly fixing the configuration values or further incorporating new security alternatives.

3.2 AMI Security Analysis

This section presents the formal model corresponding to the AMI security verification. Then, it describes the implementation of this formal model along with necessary demonstrations using examples.

3.2.1 Preliminary

Figure 1.3 in Chap. 1 presents a typical AMI topology. An example of the AMI configuration are partially shown in Figs. 3.2 and 3.3. This sample data consists of the device configurations, topology, communication between the devices, data delivery schedules in the network, etc. The device configurations are modeled using an abstraction model. The abstraction is done by exploiting the correlation between the configuration parameters of different AMI devices, as there is often a very large number of smart meters in a smart grid. The organizational requirements and various security guidelines (e.g., NISTIR) are modeled as invariant and user-driven constraints.

Meter Class	ID	Type	Patch Info	Sampling Info	Reporting Mode (to Collector)	Report Schedule	Auth Property	Encrypt Property	Ports in Service	Comm Protocol
meter	m00003	ge	pm011, pm115	18,40	push	15,40	auth1	encrypt1	nil	lontalk
meter	m00123	echelon	pm115	15,30	push	20,30	auth0	encrypt1	nil	lontalk
meter	m00129	echelon	pm115	20,30	push	20,60	auth1	encrypt1	nil	lontalk

Collector Class	ID	Type	Patch Info	Buffer Info	Reporting Mode (to Headend)	Schedule (to	Pull Schedule (from meter)	ConnectedMeters	Connected Headend	Link (to Meter)	Auth Property	Encrypt Property	Ports in Service	Comm Protocol
collector	c0003	rev03	pc213, pc012	data, 9000, 1	pull	nil	nil	m00003,5; m00123,4	hs001	powerline1	auth1, auth2	encrypt1, encrypt2	22, 53, 161, 222	lontalk, ip
collector	c0005	rev02	pc012	data, 8000, 1	push	300, 14400	nil	m00003,5; m00129,5	hs001	powerline1	auth1, auth2	encrypt1, encrypt2	22, 53, 161, 222	lontalk, ip

Headend Class	ID	Type	OS	Patch Info	Pull Schedule (from Collector)	Auth Property	Encrypt Property	Ports in Service	Comm Protocol
headend	hs001	nil	win2010	p357, p254	180, 2880, c0003	auth2, none	encrypt2, none	22, 53, 161	ip

Backend Class	ID	OS	Patch	Auth Property	Encrypt Property	Ports in Service	Comm Protocol
backend	bs001	fedora14	p357	none	none	22	ip

Home Host Class	ID	OS	Auth Property	Encrypt Property	Ports in Service	Comm Protocol
home host	h0001	win_vista	none	none	—	ip

Fig. 3.2 An example data of the AMI device configurations

Link	Src	Dest	Status	Link Type			
link	zc101	v1	up	gprs			
link	zhs101	r2	up	ethernet1			
link	v1	r1	up	fiber1			
Link Profile	**ID**	**Media**	**Mode**	**Shared Status**	**BW**		
link profile	powerline1	power_line	halfduplex	yes	5		
link profile	wifi1	wireless	fullduplex	no	150		
Auth Profile	**ID**	**Algo**	**Key**				
auth	auth0	sha1	96				
auth	auth1	sha1	160				
auth	auth_ipsec1	sha1	160				
Encrypt Profile	**ID**	**Algorithm**	**Key**				
encrypt	encrypt1	rc4	64				
encrypt	encrypt2	rc4	128				
encrypt	crypt_ipsec1	md5	64				
Fw Policy	**Node**	**Src**	**Src Port**	**Dest**	**Dest Port**	**Protocol**	**Action**	**Limit**
fw policy	f1	150.0.0.0/8	161	172.16.0.0/16	161	udp	allow	_
fw policy	f1	150.0.0.0/8	22	172.16.0.0/16	22	tcp	allow	_

Fig. 3.3 An example data of AMI topology configuration

3.2.2 Formal Model of AMI Security Verification

The modeling of AMI security verification has two parts: (1) AMI system (configurations) model and (2) threat analysis model.

3.2.2.1 AMI Configuration Model

The modeling of the AMI configuration includes AMI physical devices, the topology, and communication and security properties.

Modeling of AMI Physical Components The formalization of different AMI physical devices primarily includes smart meters, intelligent data collectors, and the headend system. A logical abstraction is applied for modeling the AMI configuration.

Configuration Level Abstraction An enterprise smart grid network typically consists of millions of smart meters and thousands of collectors distributed over different geographical regions. In order to perform data delivery, these devices communicate with each other based on device configurations and communication properties. For the purpose of achieving better scalability, the idea of configuration level abstraction is applied that leverages the similarities between configurations of the devices. According to this abstraction, different classes are defined for each kind of devices. A particular class of devices shares the same (physical and logical) configuration properties. This abstraction is not limited with this class-based concept within meters and collectors. In order to have a common design model, the same concept is applied for all kinds of AMI devices. However, the cyber-physical devices (e.g., routers, firewalls, etc.) are not modeled as classes. Since these classes do not associated with network identities (i.e., IP addresses), the concept of *zone* is also applied. A zone is a collection of similar (but not only limited to same class) AMI devices and provide network identity (usually subnet-based) to the zone. These zones are formed only for collectors.

Table 3.1 Formal definition of a meter and a collector

Smart Meter:

$SM_i \rightarrow Type_i \wedge Patch_i \wedge SRate_i \wedge Mode_i \wedge RSche_i \wedge$
$\quad\quad Auth_i \wedge Encr_i \wedge Serv_i \wedge CommProto_i \wedge TRate_i$

$Patch_i \rightarrow \bigwedge_{j=0...} Patch_{i,j}$

$SRate_i \rightarrow SSize_i \wedge STime_i$

$RSche_i \rightarrow RScheBase_i \wedge RScheInt_i$

$Auth_i \rightarrow \bigwedge_{j=0...} (AAlgo_{i,j} \wedge AKey_{i,j})$

$Encr_i \rightarrow \bigwedge_{j=0...} (EAlgo_{i,j} \wedge EKey_{i,j})$

$Serv_i \rightarrow \bigwedge_{j=0...} SPort_{i,j}$

$CommProto_i \rightarrow \bigwedge_{j=0...} CommProto_{i,j}$

Intelligent Data Collector:

$IC_i \rightarrow Type_i \wedge Patch_i \wedge BufSize_i \wedge Mode_i \wedge RSche_i \wedge$
$\quad\quad PRSche_i \wedge Auth_i \wedge Encr_i \wedge AttachSM_i \wedge LinkToSM_i \wedge$
$\quad\quad AttachHS_i \wedge Serv_i \wedge CommProto_i \wedge TRate_i$

. . . .

$PRSche_i \rightarrow \bigwedge_{j=0...} (PScheBase_{i,j} \wedge PScheInt_{i,j} \wedge RDev_{i,j})$

$ConnSM_i \rightarrow \bigwedge_{j=0...} (CSMId_{i,j} \wedge CSMNum_{i,j})$

Smart Meter A meter class is identified by an ID. Its profile *SM* is represented as
a conjunction ($\wedge$) of different parameters as shown in Table 3.1. The vendor type
(i.e., *Echelon*, *GE*, etc.) is represented by parameter *Type*. The sampling information
of a meter is represented using *SInfo* that consists of two components: sampling
size (*SSize* in KB) and sampling time (*STime*). A meter can deliver data to a
collector in two different modes: pull and push. In pull mode, the meter reports
data based on the request from the collector that follows a specific pull schedule
of the collector. On the other hand, in push mode, the meter reports data to the
collector (without waiting for a request) based on its own report schedule. This
reporting mode is captured by *Mode*. The reporting time schedule of a meter (in
push mode) is modeled using *RSche* that consists of *RScheBase* and *RScheInt*. This
indicates that the meter will report periodically in a regular interval of *RScheInt*
starting from *RScheBase* after the base time. To achieve end-to-end security, the
communicating devices must agree in their cryptographic (i.e., authentication and
encryption) properties. The authentication properties of a meter is modeled using
parameter *Auth* as conjunction of algorithm (*AAlgo*) and key length (*AKey*). A meter
may support multiple authentication properties. The encryption property is modeled
similarly as *Encr*. The running services and communication protocols associated
with a meter are represented by *Serv* and *CommProto*, respectively. Parameter *Patch*

denotes the patches that are installed in the meter. The maximum transmission rate (in Mbps) of a meter is denoted by *TRate*. The formalization of a meter class is shown in Table 3.1.

Intelligent Data Collector A collector class profile *IC* is represented as a conjunction of different parameters, which include all those of the meter class profile except the sampling information. In addition, each collector may have a pull schedule that is represented by parameter *PRSche*. It has three components: *PSBTime*, *PInt*, and *RDev*, which denote that the collector periodically pulls data from a reporting device (*RDev*, a meter) starting at *PScheBase* with interval *PScheInt*. A collector has a buffer for storing the report data from different meters. *BufSize* represents the buffer size (in KB). The parameter *ConnSM* is a conjunction of meter classes (*CSMId*) and their numbers (*CSMNum*), and they represent the meters connected to the collector. *LinkToSM* represents the ID of the link that connects the collector to the meter. Parameter *AttachHS* represents the headend system to which data is reported by the collector.

Headend System A headend system class profile *HS* is a conjunction of various parameters: *Type*, *OS*, *Mode*, *TRate*, *Patch*, *PRSche*, *Auth*, *Encr*, *Serv*, and *CommProto*. These properties are modeled as similar to those of meter and collector.

Host Devices An AMI network contains different types of hosts, such as (1) hosts of home area network (enterprise clients), (2) enterprise internal hosts, (3) enterprise application servers (backend systems), and (4) external hosts from the Internet. Hosts have considerably less parameters. For example, an enterprise client host class profile has *OS*, *Auth*, *Encr*, *Serv*, *CommProto*, and *TRate* parameters only.

Modeling of AMI Topology AMI topology defines the physical and logical connectivity between different AMI and network devices.

Router, Firewall and IPSec Devices The router (*R*), firewall (*F*), and IPSec (*IS*) devices are modeled similar to the idea considered in [2]. The traffic limiting capability of a firewall is modeled using parameter *FwLim* along with its action (*FwAct*) in its policy (*FwPolicy*). A router selects the next-hop (*RNext*) for a particular traffic based on its forwarding policy (*RPolicy*).

Link A link is identified by an ID (*LId*). Its profile is a conjunction of *NodePair* (i.e., the node-pair connected by the link) and *LinkStatus* (i.e., up or down). *LId* binds the specified link type to parameter *LinkProp* that represents the properties of that link including *MediaType* (i.e., wireless, ethernet, etc.), *SharedStatus* (i.e., shared or not), *CommMode* (i.e., half-duplex, full-duplex, etc.), and *LinkBw* (in Mbps).

Zone Each zone has an ID. The profile of a zone (*Zone*) is comprised of three parameters: *ZSn*, *ZMem*, and *ZGw*. The parameter *ZSn* denotes an IP-address (with subnet Mask) that covers all devices in that zone. *ZMem* represents the IDs of different device classes and the number of devices (that belong to the zone) under

Table 3.2 Modeling of a zone and its relation with AMI devices

Zone:

$Zone_i \rightarrow ZSn_i \wedge ZMem_i \wedge ZGw_i$

$ZSn_i \rightarrow Ip_{i,j} \wedge Mask_{i,j}$

$ZMem_{i,j} \rightarrow ZMId_{i,j} \wedge ZMNum_{i,j}$

. . . .

$ZMem_i \rightarrow \bigwedge_{j=0\ldots} ZMem_{i,j}$

Representation of a source:

$(S \rightarrow Id \wedge ZId) \rightarrow (Id = ZMId)$

each class. *ZGw* denotes the gateway router ID for that zone. The formalization of a zone, $Zone_i$ is represented in Table 3.2. The source or destination node of a traffic flow is represented as a conjunction of its ID (*Id*) and its zone's ID (*ZId*). The number of traffic sources or destinations depends on the number of zones and the number of classes in the zones. For example, if there are 50 zones and 4 collector classes per zone on average, then there are 200 possible collectors, as either source or destination. A source or destination with respect to a traffic, in this model, is referred to a node associated with its zone. Note that a group of meters is directly associated with a collector, thus addressable through this collector.

3.2.2.2 AMI Threat Verification Model

Appropriate modeling of the constraints is required to identify security threats on AMI. These constraints are classified into invariant and user-driven constraints, many of which are mapped to the NISTIR [10] guidelines.

Modeling of Invariant Constraints There are various invariant constraints based on connectivity, data delivery schedule, resource availability, etc. between AMI components. These constraints must be satisfied for any successful communication.

Reachability Constraint Reachability must hold between a pair of devices, if data is required to be transmitted between them. For example, a meter should be able to reach a collector to deliver the report to the collector. Similarly, there should be reachability from collector to the headend system, so that the collector can deliver the report to the headend. This constraint intuitively verifies the links between a pair of devices for the satisfaction of routing and security device policies. The formalization of general reachability constraint is shown in Table 3.3. The formalization defines *Forward* to check whether a specific traffic $Tr_{S,D}$ (i.e., from *S* to *D*) can be transferred from a node (*X*) to another node (*Y*) (like state transition). Then, *Reachable* and the reachability constraint (*ReachabilityConstr*) are defined

Table 3.3 Formalizations of reachability and pairing constraints

---

Reachability Constraint:

$Forward_{X,Y,Trs_D,TrR} \rightarrow$

$\quad Link_{X,Y} \wedge$

$\quad (((X = S) \wedge (ZGw_S = Y)) \vee (Y = D) \vee$

$\quad\quad (R_X \wedge RPolicy_{X,Trs_D} \wedge (RNext_X = Y)) \wedge$

$\quad\quad ((F_X \rightarrow FwPolicy_{X,Trs_D} \wedge FwAct_X \wedge$

$\quad\quad\quad (FwLim \rightarrow (TrR = min(LimVal, LinkBw_{X,Y})))) \vee$

$\quad\quad\quad (\neg F_X \rightarrow (TrR = LinkBw_{X,Y})))$

$Reachable_{A,B,Trs_D,TrR} \rightarrow$

$\quad Forward_{A,B,Trs_D,TrR} \vee$

$\quad (\exists C, Forward_{A,C,Trs_D,TrR1} \wedge Reachable_{C,B,Trs_D,TrR2} \wedge$

$\quad\quad (TrR = min(TrR1, TrR2))$

$ReachabilityConstr_{Trs_D,TrR} \rightarrow Reachable_{S,D,Trs_D,TrR}$

Pairing Constraint:

$AuthPairing_{S,D} \rightarrow$

$\quad (AAlgo_S = AAlgo_D) \wedge (AKey_S = AKey_D)$

$EncrPairing_{S,D} \rightarrow$

$\quad (EAlgo_S = EAlgo_D) \wedge (EKey_S = EKey_{m,D})$

$ProtoPairing_{S,D} \rightarrow$

$\quad (Proto \in CommProto_S) \wedge (Proto \in CommProto_D)$

$PairingConstr_{S,D} \rightarrow$

$\quad AuthPairing_{S,D} \wedge EncrPairing_{S,D} \wedge ProtoPairing_{S,D}$

---

on top of this. In the constraint formalization, the maximum possible transmission rate (TrR) is considered by taking the minimum bandwidth of the links across the path along with the limits that may be imposed by a firewall.

Pairing Constraint Consistent pairing between a meter and a collector is required over reachability for successful communication. This constraint is considered as a conjunction of security-pairing and protocol-pairing. In other words, it states that the authentication and confidentiality properties of the communicating devices should match and they have a common protocol to communicate. For example, in Fig. 3.2, although there are 4 m of class $m000123$ connected with collector $c0003$, they are not allowed to communicate as the security-pairing will be violated due to a mismatch in their authentication properties (i.e., $auth0$ and $auth1$). Similarly, a host from HAN will not be able to communicate with a meter if that host does not support the LonTalk protocol, which is the only protocol supported by a meter. $PairingConstr$ in Table 3.3 checks these issues.

Table 3.4 Formalizations of schedule and resource constraints

---

Schedule Constraints:

$MeterSampConstr_M \rightarrow$
$\quad SM_M \wedge (Mode_M \rightarrow ((STime_M \leq RScheInt_M) \wedge$
$\quad\quad (RScheBase_M \leq RScheInt_M))) \wedge$
$\quad\quad ((SSize_M / STime_M) \leq TRate_M)$

$CollectorPullScheConstr_C \rightarrow$
$\quad IC_C \wedge (((M = CSMId_C) \wedge \neg Mode_M) \rightarrow PRSche_C)$

Resource Constraints:

$(TotalSData_C = \sum_M SData_M) \rightarrow$
$\quad (M = CSMId_C) \rightarrow$
$\quad\quad (SData_M = (SSize_M \times CSMNum_C)))$
$CollectorBufConstr_C \rightarrow$
$\quad IC_C \wedge (BufSize_C \geq TotalSData_C)$

$(TotalSRate_C = \sum_M SRate_M) \rightarrow$
$\quad (M = CSMId_C) \wedge$
$\quad\quad (SRate_M = ((SSize_M / STime_M) \times CSMNum_C)))$
$CollectorTrRConstr_C \rightarrow$
$\quad IC_C \wedge (TrR_C \geq TotalSRate_C)$
$CollectorBwOutConstr_C \rightarrow$
$\quad IC_C \wedge (TotalSRate_C \leq LinkBw_{C,ZGw_C})$

Schedule Constraint The schedule constraints (Table 3.4) ensure the basic correctness of the report or pull schedule configuration. The *MeterSampConstr* constraint states that the sampling time and the reporting base-start time of a meter must be less than or equal to its reporting interval, such that no reporting is done without new data. It also verifies that the sampling rate cannot be more than its maximum transmission rate. If a meter is in push mode (*Mode* is true), then it should have a reporting schedule. A similar constraint (*CollectorPullScheConstr*) is true for a collector. If a collector is connected with some meters, whose reporting modes are pull (*Mode* is false), then the collector should have a pull schedule for them.

Resource Constraint There are different resource constraints (Table 3.4), which are often related to report/pull schedules. The *CollectorBufConsrt* constraint states that the buffer size of a collector should be greater than or equal to the cumulative sampled data size of all the meters connected to that collector. Otherwise, data loss must occur in the collector buffer under any report schedule. Similarly, the *CollectorTrRateConstr* constraint states that the cumulative sampling rate of the connected meters cannot be more than the transmission rate of the collector. The *CollectorBwConstr* constraint states that the bandwidth of the link from the

Table 3.5 Formalizations of different user-driven constraints

---

Data Overwrite Protection Constraint:

$(TotalRData_C = TotalSRate_C \times Period) \rightarrow$

$\quad ((Mode_C \rightarrow (Period = RSInt_C)) \vee$

$\quad\quad (\neg Mode_C \rightarrow (H = AttachHS_C) \wedge (Period = PRSInt_H)))$

$OverwriteProtectConstr_C \rightarrow$

$\quad IC_C \wedge (BufSize_C \geq TotalRData_C)$

Cyber Bandwidth Constraint:

$(Num_C = \sum_Z ZMNum_Z) \rightarrow (MId_Z = C)$

$(TotalRRate_{H,Sche} = \sum_C (TotalSRate_C \times Num_C)) \rightarrow$

$\quad (H = AttachHS_C) \wedge Mode_C \wedge (RSche_C = Sche)$

$LinkBwConstr_{H,X,Y} \rightarrow$

$\quad HS_H \wedge (LinkBw_{X,Y} \geq TotalRRate_H)$

Assured Data Delivery Constraint:

$AssuredDelivery_{M,C,H} \rightarrow$

$\quad SM_M \wedge IC_C \wedge HS_H \wedge$

$\quad Pairing_{M,C} \wedge (M = CSMId_C) \wedge Reachable_{M,C} \wedge$

$\quad Pairing_{C,H} \wedge (H = AttacheHS_C) \wedge Reachable_{C,H} \wedge$

$\quad ResourceConstr_{M,C,H} \wedge CyberConstr_{M,C,H}$

Quality of Delivery (Data Freshness) Constraint:

$FreshnessConstr_{M,C,H,T} \rightarrow$

$\quad AssuredDelivery_{M,C,H} \wedge$

$\quad ((Sum_{T1,T2} \leq T) \rightarrow$

$\quad\quad (((T1 = RSInt_M) \wedge Mode_M) \vee ((T1 = PRSInt_C) \wedge \neg Mode_M)) \wedge$

$\quad\quad (((T2 = RSInt_C) \wedge Mode_C) \vee ((T2 = PRSInt_H) \wedge \neg Mode_C))$

Availability Protection Constraint (Limit DoS Attack):

$(MaxTrR_{H,X,Y} = \sum_C TrR_C \times Num_C) \rightarrow$

$\quad Compromise_C \wedge (AttachHS_C = H) \wedge Forward_{X,Y,TrC,H,TrR}$

$AvailProtectionConstr_{H,X,Y} \rightarrow$

$\quad IC_C \wedge (LinkBw_{X,Y} \geq MaxTrR_{H,X,Y})$

---

collector to its gateway must be greater than or equal to the accumulated sampling rate of all the meters connected to it. Otherwise, no schedule will be possible without data loss.

Modeling of User-Driven Constraints To achieve correct and secure functioning of the AMI network, there can exist different user-driven constraints. In this discussion, AMI-specific constraints are considered. Formalizations of these constraints are shown in Table 3.5.

Data Overwrite Protection Constraint This constraint states that the aggregate report data of all the meters connected to a specific collector must not flood the collector buffer within the reporting interval [5, 12]. For example, in Fig. 3.2, collector

$c0005$ receives reports from 5 m of class $m00129$ (sampling rate: 20 KB/30 s) and 5 m of the $m0003$ class (sampling rate: 18 KB/40 s). Therefore, $c0005$ will receive 335 KB (average) data every 60 s, which is to be stored in its buffer. Based on the report schedule, the collector pushes the data to the headend every 1440 s. Thus, during this period, an aggregate of 8040 KB data will be sent to the collector by these meters. This amount of data will flood the collector buffer (size 8000 KB), which will in turn cause data loss (i.e., initial 40 KB report data will be overwritten).

Cyber Bandwidth Constraint The *LinkBwConstr* constraint is to confirm that the aggregate report rate of collectors reporting simultaneously due to matching report schedule should not exceed the bandwidth limitation of the network path (considering a link from X to Y) connecting to the headend (H). A violation of this constraint will cause link congestion or distributed DoS (DDoS).

Assured Data Delivery Constraint This constraint requires checking the end-to-end data delivery (from a meter to the headend through a collector) to satisfy the AMI global functionality. This constraint intuitively implies the satisfaction of the following constraints: (1) reachability, (2) successful security-pairing, (3) availability of resources (conjunction of all resource constraints including data overwrite constraint as *ResourceConstr*), and (4) synchronous reporting without flooding the cyber toward the headend. A violation of these constraints can create failure in data delivery.

Quality-of-Delivery Constraint There are user-driven constraints for ensuring the quality of delivery. For example, the report freshness constraint (*FreshnessConstr*) restricts the delivery of data within a specific time window along with assured data delivery. A user can have a quality requirement on trusted paths. For example, this requirement can be defined as the satisfaction of (1) end-to-end encryption level based on key length (e.g., 256 bits); and (2) specific single or nested tunnels (e.g., 2-level nested tunnels) requirements.

Availability Protection Constraint This constraint (*AvailProtectionConstr*) ensures that if there are X number (or portion) of AMI devices being compromised, the assured data delivery constraint is still preserved. It intuitively verifies that DoS attack is not possible on links or endpoints, when the number of compromised nodes is no more than X (say, 5 % collectors).

3.2.3 Implementation

3.2.3.1 SMT Encoding and Constraint Verification

The implementation of this framework primarily includes the encoding of the formalizations discussed above into SMT logics. The parameters used in the formalizations are encoded using mainly Boolean, integer, and bit-vector terms. Boolean terms are used to encode the Boolean configuration parameters. The remaining parameters are modeled as integer terms. The parameters that may take real values (e.g., bandwidth) are normalized into integers. Bit-vector (or bit-array) terms, which are capable to handle bitwise operations on numbers, are used for encoding IP addresses. It is worth mentioning that some of the arithmetic computations used in the formalizations require multiplying or dividing two variables. SMT solvers that do not support such non-linear operations cannot be used as the SMT model solving engine for the framework. Since Z3 SMT solver [3] has this capability, this framework employs this solver. After defining the configuration parameters as SMT variables, the constraints are encoded. The verification query is the satisfaction of one or more constraints with the configuration model. For example, if M_{Conf} and M_{Constr} are the AMI configuration and constraint models respectively, the verification query Q is encoded as $Q \rightarrow M_{Conf} \wedge M_{Constr}$.

The SMT solver generates the verification results, which are either *sat* (satisfiable) or *unsat* (unsatisfiable). In the case of an *unsat*, the verification engine provides an *unsat-core* that basically represents the traces of constraint violations in the configuration. Then, the Diagnoser module, which is discussed later, systematically examines these violation traces and generates a comprehensive threat report. This report includes threat sources, targets, violating rules and reasonings, and a remediation plan showing possible reconfigurations for hardening the system with respect to the identified problems. Leveraging the Z3 APIs for rich languages like C/C++, C#, and Python, an integrated program is developed for the Parser module to read the configuration from the input file, encode the model into SMT, and solve it.

3.2.3.2   Methodology of Unsatisfied-Core Generation

If the SMT solver gives an *unsat* result, it is possible to produce an *unsat-core* from the solver, which describes the unsatisfied constraints that are unsatisfied. The unsatisfied constraints specify the corresponding configurations parameters that are candidate for this unsatisfaction. In order to get the *unsat-core*, the concept of *hard* and *soft* clauses (a verification of assumptions in Z3) are used. Therefore, configurations and associated constraints are separated into these two groups. The fixed properties are often considered as hard clauses, while the rest as assumptions or soft clauses. If the model verification fails, the *unsat-core* shows the list of assumptions, i.e., the constraints (and the configurations), which are not satisfied. From the list of the unsatisfied configurations, it is possible to trace the reasoning of a constraint failure.

3.2.3.3   Methodology of Remediation Plan Synthesis

In order to get a remediation plan, it is required to have a policy for the reconfigurations. The policy shows feasible or preferred invariant and user-driven guidelines for possible reconfiguration candidates. An invariant guideline represents the configurations that are practically infeasible to modify. The vendor specific device configurations (such as the buffer size of a collector) are usually constant for a device. Hence, changing this property requires replacing the device with a different or newer product that has the required configuration property. The user-driven guidelines represent the organizational priorities or capabilities for performing reconfigurations. For example, the organization may be fine with deploying many collectors, but a minimum number of meters must be connected to each collector.

In the process of exploring the reconfiguration plan, the diagnoser module continuously checks the satisfaction of the model by releasing the assumptions (soft clauses) of the configurations systematically according to the remediation guidelines until the model verification gives a *sat* result. Releasing an assumption lets the solver choose the configuration values associated with the assumption that satisfy the hard clauses along with the remaining assumptions. This process is an implementation of *max-sat* [9]. Then, a remediation plan is generated from the *max-sat* output. It is worth mentioning that if quantifiers are required to use for the purpose of verifying some constraints, Z3 may return *unknown* instead of *sat*. This implies that there is no constraint violation found by the solver. Hence, if the result is not *unsat*, it can be assumed that the model is satisfied with the given constraints.

3.2.3.4 Verification Trace Analysis: An Example

This section describes how verification traces (results) from the SMT solver are analyzed to find the causes of constraint violations, along with the remediation plans for them. The procedure is explained using an example that demonstrates the collector resource (buffer) constraint. Table 3.6 shows the SMT-LIB encoding of the AMI configuration (required segment only) and the collector resource constraint (refer to Table 3.4). To comprehend the verification trace, a tiny AMI configuration is considered with 2 m, one collector, and one headend system. Here, the constraint verification gives a *sat* result. This signifies that the AMI configuration satisfies the resource constraint. Thus, there is no *unsat-core* in this evaluation. However, an *unsat* result is received when the AMI configuration model is modified by setting the buffer size to a reduced value, 100 KB.

The experiment's result is presented in Table 3.7. It shows that there is no model that satisfies the collector resource constraint. It also shows the *unsat-core*, i.e., the unsatisfied constraints (assumptions). To find a *sat* result, the next step is to run the *max-sat* implementation on the configuration model sequentially by intuitively weakening the configuration constraint following the *unsat-core*. This is done by removing one predicate (among the predicates of the *unsat-core*) from the configuration constraint each time and running the model verification until the verification result converges to *sat*. The resultant satisfiable model indicates the configurations that satisfy the resource constraint. Then, the immediately preceding *unsat* trace is considered as the potential cause of the constraint violation. For example, Table 3.7 shows that the resource constraint (*PC*) is satisfied with the configuration predicates *P0* and *P1*. In this case, the number of the type 0 m and that of the type 1 m are respectively 6 and 0. The immediately preceding *unsat-core*

Table 3.6 An example of resource constraint verification

(assert (M 0)) ;; Meter 1 (Id 0)
(assert (= (Id 0) 0))
(assert (= (SSize 0) 25))
(assert (= (SInt 0) 45))

(assert (M 1)) ;; Meter 2 (Id 1)
(assert (= (MId 1) 1))
(assert (= (SSize 1) 15))
(assert (= (SInt 1) 30))

(assert (IC 10)) ;; Collector 1 (Id 10)
(assert (= (Id 10) 10))
(assert (= (BufSize 10) 200))
(assert (=> P0 (= (CSMId 10 0) 1)))
(assert (=> P1 (= (CSMId 10 1) 0)))
(assert (=> P2 (= (CSMNum 10 0) 8)))
(assert (=> P3 (= (CSMNum 10 1) 8)))

(assert (=> PC
  (=> (CollectorBufConstr 10)
    (and (M (CSMId 10 0)) (M (CSMId 10 1))
      (= (SData 10 0) (* (CSMNum 10 0) (SSize (CSMId 10 0))))
      (= (SData 10 1) (* (CSMNum 10 1) (SSize (CSMId 10 1))))
      (>= (BufSize 10) (+ (SData 10 0) (SData 10 1)))))))

(assert (CollectorBufConstr 1))

(check-sat PC P0 P1 P2 P3) ;; Sat
(get-model)
(get-unsat-core) ;; Unsuccessful

---

is "*PC P0 P1 P2*", which indicates that the predicate *P2* leads the violation. It can be observed that the predicate *P2* in the configuration (as shown in Table 3.6) asserts the number of each type of meters as 8, which leads to the unsatisfiability of the resource constraint when the buffer size is 100 KB.

From the *unsat-core*, it is found that the remediation to the collector resource constraint violation is possible by applying one of the following measures: (1) changing the collector's buffer size, (2) changing the sampling size or rate of the meter(s), and (3) changing the number of meters to transmit data to the collector. The buffer size of a collector is basically vendor-specific and this is not configurable except by replacing the collector with a different one (having a larger buffer). This is an example of invariant guidelines, which specifies that the collector's buffer size

Table 3.7 An example of the diagnosis process

Modified Model:

. . . .

(assert (= (BufSize 10) 100))

. . . .

(check-sat PC P0 P1 P2 P3) ;; Unsat

(get-unsat-core)

Solver Output:

unsat

(P0 P1 P2 P3 PC)

Max-SAT Implementation:

. . . .

(assert (forall ((c Int) (x Int))

   (=> (and (>= c 10) (<= c 10) (>= x 0) (<= x 1))

    (and (>= (CSMId c x) 0) (<= (CSMId c x) 1)))))

(assert (forall ((c Int) (x Int))

   (=> (and (>= c 10) (<= c 10))

    (>= (+ (CSMNum c 0) (CSMNum c 1)) 6)

    (>= (CSMNum c 0) 0) (>= (CSMNum c 1) 0))))

. . . .

(check-sat P0 P1 P2 PC) ;; Unsat

(get-model) ;; Unsuccessful

(get-unsat-core) ;; (P0 P1 P2 PC)

. . . .

(check-sat P0 P1 PC) ;; Sat

(get-model) ;; Successful

(get-unsat-core) ;; Unsuccessful

Satisfied Model:

. . . .

CSMNum − > {

   10 1 − > 6 ;; The number of type 1 m is 6

   else − > 0} ;; The number other type (type 0) meter is 0

. . . .

---

cannot be considered in the remediation plan. The sampling rate of a meter is also vendor-specific. However, it might be possible to replace a meter with a different one (chosen from the available meters) that has a smaller sampling size or rate. Hence, in this example the (numbers of) meters connected to the collector are considered as assumptions (the predicates $P0$ and $P1$). It is easy to change the number of meters

connected to the collector. Two assumptions, *P2* and *P3*, are taken corresponding
to the number of meters. However, in the diagnosis process, it could be possible to
assume that the organization is using only one vendor-specific type of meter (e.g.,
the type 0 m) and presently the organization is not willing to try different vendors.
This is an example of user-driven guidelines, when the *P2* and *P3* assumptions
cannot be considered.

3.3   SCADA Security Analysis

This section presents the formal model corresponding to SCADA security requirements and demonstrate the model with an example illustrating the verification of a
requirement.

3.3.1   Preliminary

Figure 1.5 in Chap. 1 presents a SCADA topology. Figure 3.4 shows a sample
SCADA configuration that partially represents the SCADA system with regards to
the physical components, the topology, and the communication and security properties. Such a template file serves as the input to the security analysis framework.

IED	ID	Type	Report Mode	Ports in Service	ICS Protocol	MAC Address	IP Address	Patch Info	Measurements
ied	i0001	sel	pull	nil	modbus	00:0a:95:9d:68:16	-	pi001, pil43	9
ied	i0012	abb	pull	nil	dnp3	-	150.12.0.12	pi034	21, 22

PLC	ID	Type	Report Mode	Ports in Service	ICS Protocol	Operating System	MAC Address	IP Address	Patch Info
plc	p0003	siemens	pull	nil	dnp3	vxWorks	-	150.1.10.02	pp031, pp113
plc	p0005	sel	pull	nil	dnp3, modbus	os-9	-	150.11.0.34	pp140

RTU	ID	Type	OS	Ports in Service	ICS Protocol	MAC Address	IP Address	Patch
rtu	r001	sel	freeRTOS	nil	dnp3, modbus	00:A0:C9:14:C8:29	150.1.0.101	pr208

MTU	ID	OS	Ports in Service	ICS Protocol	MAC Address	IP Address	Patch
mtu	m01	linux	22	dnp3, modbus	-	150.2.50.51	p322

Internal Host	ID	OS	Ports in Service	Comm Protocol	MAC Address	IP Address	Patch
ent-host	h0001	windows-7	-	ip	-	150.200.20.64	p357

Link	End 1	End 2	Status	Link Type
link	i0001	r001	up	ethernet
link	p0003	r001	up	ethernet
link	r001	m01	up	gprs

Link Profile	ID	Media	Shared Status	BW
link profile	ethernet	wired	yes	10
link profile	modem	wireless	no	0.028

Crypto Property	Device ID	Source ID	Destination ID	Crypto Type
crypto prop	i0001	i0001	-	crypt3
crypto prop	p0003	p0003	-	crypt3, crypt4
crypto prop	r001	r001	i0001	crypt1
crypto prop	r001	r001	m01	crypt5, crypt6

Crypto Profile	ID	Algo	Key Length
crypto	crypt1	hmac-sha1	128
crypto	crypt2	hmac-sha256	256
crypto	crypt3	chap	64
crypto	crypt4	sha2	128
crypto	crypt5	rsa	1024
crypto	crypt6	aes	128
crypto	crypt7	tls	1024, 128

Fig. 3.4   An example data of the SCADA configuration

It is worth mentioning that, unlike the framework for AMI, no abstraction is used to model SCADA devices (i.e., the data communicating field devices like IEDs, RTUs, and PLCs), because they are limited in number compared to smart meters in AMI. The SCADA configuration and security guidelines are formally modeled as constraints and encodes these constraints into SMT logics. Then, these constraints are verified using the Z3 SMT solver [3] and a violation of these constraints is identified as a threat. The generation of necessary remediation plans for identified threats specific to SCADA follows the same process as it presented in Sect. 3.2.3.4.

3.3.2 Formal Model of SCADA Security Verification

The formal modeling for the SCADA security verification has two parts: the modeling of the SCADA configuration and that of the security requirements.

3.3.2.1 SCADA Configuration Model

A SCADA network consists of different types of devices, heterogeneous communication links, and various access control and security policies. The formalizations of these the SCADA configuration are similar to those of the AMI configuration. Therefore, this section only presents some selective formalizations of these configurations.

Modeling of SCADA Physical Components SCADA consists of different physical device components, among which IEDs, PLCs, RTUs, and MTUs are important. Usually IEDs, PLCS, RTUs, and PMUs are associated with substations, while an MTU is associated with a control center. IEDs, PLCs, and RTUs are referred to as field devices. Each SCADA physical device is modeled based on its parameters, as shown in Fig. 3.4. The modeling of physical devices are similar to that of AMI physical devices, except it does not use the class-based abstraction in modeling the field devices. The modeling of an RTU is presented in the below, while the other devices have similar modeling.

The formalization of an RTU is shown in Table 3.8. An RTU is identified by an ID. Its profile *Rtu* is represented as a conjunction of different parameters. Parameter *Type* represents the vendor type (e.g., ABB, SEL, and Siemens) of the RTU. Although an RTU typically delivers data (measurements) to the control server (i.e., MTU, residing at the control center) upon receiving a request from the server, both of the possible reporting modes, pull and push, are considered. This is captured by *Mode*. The reporting time schedule of an RTU is modeled similarly to a smart meter or a collector. To achieve end-to-end security, the communicating devices must agree in their cryptographic (authentication and encryption) properties. The cryptographic properties are modeled using *Crypt* as a conjunction of algorithm (*CAlgo*) and key length (*CKey*). A device often supports multiple cryptographic

Table 3.8 Formal (partial) definition of a remote terminal unit

Remote Terminal Unit (RTU):

$RTU_i \rightarrow Type_i \wedge Patch_i \wedge Mode_i \wedge Crypt_i \wedge OS_i \wedge Serv_i \wedge$
$\quad ICommProto_i \wedge MAC_i \wedge Ip_i$

$Patch_i \rightarrow \bigwedge_{j=0...} Patch_{i,j}$

$Crypt_i \rightarrow \bigwedge_{j=0...} (CAlgo_{i,j} \wedge CKey_{i,j})$

$Serv_i \rightarrow \bigwedge_{j=0...} SPort_{i,j}$

$ICommProto_i \rightarrow \bigwedge_{j=0...} ICommProto_{i,j}$

properties. The running services associated with an RTU are represented by *Serv*. The communication protocols are specified using *CommProto*. Typically, there are ICS-specific protocols (e.g., modbus, DNP3, etc.) for communication. Since no abstraction is used in formalizing an RTU, each RTU has a unique address. The MAC address and the IP address of an RTU are specified using *MacAddr* and *IpAddr*, respectively. Parameter *Patch* denotes the patches that are installed in the RTU.

Modeling of SCADA Topology Typically, multiple IEDs/PLCs are connected with an RTU, while all or some RTUs are connected to an MTU directly or through some intermediate RTUs and/or WAN. There can be more than a single MTU, in which case one of them works as the main MTU (corresponding to the main control center), while the rest of the MTUs are connected to the main one. The measurements and control commands flow through this communication topology between the devices. If PMUs exist in SCADA, there is usually a separate network from PMUs to MTUs through WAN, where multiple PMUs are connected to one or more intermediate PDCs and these PDCs feed data to MTUs. Usually communications to control centers (MTUs) are restricted by firewalls. Here, the modeling of a communication link is briefly discussed below.

A link in SCADA is formalized similarly to that in AMI. Identified by an ID, a link is a conjunction of *NodePair* (i.e., the nodes connected by the link), *LinkStatus* (i.e., up or down), and *LType* (i.e., ethernet, modem, etc.). *LType* binds this link with another profile corresponding to the link type. This profile consists of *LinkProp* that represents the properties of that link, including *MediaType* (i.e., wireless, ethernet, etc.), *SharedStatus* (i.e., shared or not), and *LinkBw* (in Mbps). In this topology formalization, no abstraction is applied like in the AMI topology modeling (Sect. 3.2.2.1). Thus, each of the end nodes for a link is a single node, with a specific MAC or IP address.

3.3.2.2 SCADA Threat Verification Model

The potential threats to SCADA are very similar to the threats that are seen in AMI. The security controls specified in NIST SP 800-82 [4] also comply with those specified in NISTIR [10] guidelines. As they share similar logics, most of the invariant and user-driven constraints modeled in Sect. 3.2.2 are also applicable to SCADA with no or minor modification in logics. Therefore, this section presents those security constraints that are specific to SCADA. These constraints are mainly user-driven requirements, which ensure if a SCADA control process has sufficient secure (particularly, authenticated and integrity protected) data to provide correct results in normal cases or contingencies. This section discusses three security constraints based on the observability analysis, a prior and crucial requirement for performing the power system state estimation control routine [1, 13]. These constraints are (1) secured observability, (2) k-resilient secured observability, and (3) bad data detectability. These constraints are modeled on top of another constraint, secured data delivery, similar to assured data delivery. This constraint inherently verifies different invariant constraints like reachability and security-pairing within their formalizations.

Secured Data Delivery Constraint The assured data delivery constraint verifies whether data can reach from the source to the destination, particularly a field device to the MTU through zero, one, or more intermediate devices, without ensuring whether the transmission has occurred under necessary security measures. Although this constraint checks security-pairing between the communicating parties, it is only to ensure necessary handshaking for communication. In the secured data delivery constraint (*SecuredDelivery*), it is verified that whether data is sent under proper security measures, particularly authentication and integrity protection including the assured data delivery. That is, the communicating nodes, e.g., an RTU and the MTU, may have correct security-pairing, as they are using the same security protocol, e.g., challenge-handshake authentication protocol (CHAP). However, this security-pairing on CHAP only ensures secure authentication. In this case, the transmission will not be data integrity protected. Moreover, it is required to consider the vulnerabilities of the security measures in use. For example, if DES (data encryption standard) is used for data encryption, the transmitted data cannot be considered as protected, as a good number of vulnerabilities of DES have already been found. The expert and widely accepted knowledge can be taken about the security/cryptographic measures applied to the communication in order to realize whether the data is authenticated and integrity protected. Table 3.9 shows the formalization of this constraint. Two sub-constraints, *Authenticated* and *IntegrityProtected*, are defined to facilitate this formalization by ensuring the authentication of the communicating parties and the integrity of the transmitted data, respectively.

Secured Observability Constraint The power system is observable when the measurements can solve a list of unknown variables. Each of these variables stands for a state. Typically, each measurement represents a power equation. Therefore, it

Table 3.9 Formalizations of the secured data delivery constraint for SCADA (partial)

Secured Data Delivery Constraint:

$Authenticated_{S,D} \rightarrow$
  $CryptProps_{S,D} \wedge$
  $\forall_K(K = CryptTypes_{S,D} \wedge$
    $((Algo_K = hmac \wedge KeyLength_K \geq 128) \vee \ldots))$
$IntegrityProtected_{S,D} \rightarrow$
  $CryptProps_{S,D} \wedge$
  $\forall_K(K = CryptTypes_{S,D} \wedge$
    $((Algo_K = sha2 \wedge KeyLength_K \geq 128) \vee \ldots))$
An IED is directly connected to the MTU
$SecuredDelivery_{I,M} \rightarrow$
  $Ied_I \wedge MTU_M \wedge$
  $AssuredDelivery_{I,M} \wedge Authenticated_{I,R} \wedge IntegrityProtected_{I,M}$
An IED is connected to the MTU through an RTU
$SecuredDelivery_{I,R,M} \rightarrow$
  $Ied_I \wedge Rtu_R \wedge Mtu_M \wedge$
  $AssuredDelivery_{I,R,M} \wedge Authenticated_{I,R} \wedge Authenticated_{R,M}$
  $IntegrityProtected_{I,R} \wedge IntegrityProtected_{R,M}$
Other possible communication paths from field devices toward the MTU
$SecuredDelivery_{I,R,R',M} \rightarrow$
$\ldots\ldots\ldots$

is required to each equation regarding a particular measurement, where the equation specifies the variables that produce this measurement. As it is already mentioned, the state estimation control routine is considered in this formalization. In state estimation, there is a Jacobian matrix that represents the relationships between the measurements and the unknown variables [1]. The secured observability constraint ensures two conditions: (1) the authenticated and data integrity protected distinct measurements can cover all the variables (i.e., unknown states), and (2) the number of these measurements is greater than or equal to the number of variables. These two conditions are minimal requirements to ensure that there is a secure as well as a unique solution. There are often more than one measurement that actually represents the same electrical component. For example, the power flow through a line can be measured at both ends of the line [1]. Therefore, these two measurements (forward line power flow and backward line power flow) represents the same electrical component. The formalization of this constraint is discussed below (Table 3.10).

Each row of the Jacobian matrix has a set of entries (column values), where each entry is associated with a state/variable:

Table 3.10 The input for an example of verifying secured observability in a SCADA

Number of states and measurements
5 14
Jacobian matrix (the relation between the states and the measurements)
0 -5.05 5.05 0 0
0 -5.67 0 5.67 0
0 -5.75 0 0 5.75
0 0 0 -23.75 23.75
16.9 -16.9 0 0 0
4.48 0 0 0 -4.48
0 5.67 0 -5.67 0
0 5.75 0 0 -5.75
0 0 5.85 -5.85 0
0 0 0 23.75 -23.75
-16.9 33.37 -5.05 -5.67 -5.75
0 -5.05 10.9 -5.85 0
. . . .
Number of each type of devices in the topology
IEDs (Id 1 to 8), RTUs (Id 9-12), MTU (Id 13), Router (Id 14), and Firewall (Id 15)
8 4 1 1 1
Connectivity (among the IEDs, the RTUs, and the MTU)
. . . .
Measurements corresponding to IEDs
1 1 2
2 3 5
3 11
4 12
5 4 7 9
6 13
7 6 8 10
8 14
Security profile (source, destination, applied cryptographic algorithms/keys)
11 # Number entries of security profiles
1 9 hmac 128
2 9 chap 64 sha2 128
3 9 chap 64 sha2 128
5 11 chap 64 sha2 256
6 11 chap 64 sha2 256
7 12 chap 64 sha2 128
8 12 chap 64 sha2 128
9 13 rsa 2048 aes 256
10 13 hmac 128
. . . .
k-resiliency requirements (IED, RTU)
1 1

$$
\begin{bmatrix}
h_{1,1} & h_{1,2} & \cdots & h_{1,n} \\
h_{2,1} & h_{2,2} & \cdots & h_{2,n} \\
\vdots & \vdots & \ddots & \vdots \\
h_{m,1} & h_{m,2} & \cdots & h_{m,n}
\end{bmatrix}
$$

In the matrix, $h_{i,j}$ is an entry where i is the row number associated with measurement i and j is the column number associated with variable j. This entry is often zero, i.e., the variable corresponding to this entry does not influence the measurement value associated with this row. Therefore, the variables corresponding to the nonzero entries only have impact on the measurement. Let X be a state/variable ($1 \le X \le n$), Z be a measurement ($1 \le Z \le m$), and $StateSet_Z$ be the set of states that constitute measurement Z. Then, $StateSet_Z$ is built as follows:

$$
\forall_X X \in StateSet_Z \rightarrow h_{Z,X} \neq 0
$$

If two measurements represent the same electrical components, their corresponding rows should have non-zero entries on the same columns, and they must be the same values, although the direction (sign) can be the opposite (e.g., forward and backward line power flows). Let $UMsrSet_E$ be the set of measurements that represent the same electrical component, E. These sets are built using a clustering process, where each pair of sets, $UMsrSet_E$ and $UMsrSet_{E'}$, satisfy the following property:

$$
\forall_{Z \in UMsrSet_E} \forall_{Z' \in UMsrSet_{E'}} \exists_X (h_{Z,X} \neq h_{Z',X}) \wedge (h_{Z,X} \neq -h_{Z',X})
$$

Similarly, there are power consumption measurements at buses, each of which corresponds to a particular bus. The power consumption at a bus is the summation of the all power flows incident to that bus. Thus, if all of these power flows are received as measurements, then the bus consumption measurement is redundant (i.e., not unique). This condition provides the unique bus consumption measurements.

A field device can be responsible for delivering one or more measurements. Therefore, from the mappings between communicating field devices and measurements, it is possible to logically identify which measurements are secure, while from the mappings between the measurements and the states, it can be found whether the secure measurements can observe the system. Let $IedSet$ be the set of IEDs that are responsible for taking the necessary measurements (meters/sensor data) and sending them to the MTU through an RTU. Also, let $MsrSet_I$ be the set of measurements transmitted by IED I, while S_Z be a Boolean variable denoting whether measurement Z is secure. A measurement is secure if the following two conditions hold:

$$
\forall_{I \in IedSet} \forall_{Z \in MsrSet_I} (\exists_R SecuredDelivery_{I,R,M}) \rightarrow S_Z
$$

$$
\forall_Z S_Z \rightarrow \exists_{I \in IedSet} (Z \in MsrSet_I) \wedge (\exists_R SecuredDelivery_{I,R,M})
$$

If a measurement is secured, then the variables corresponding to this measurement can be securely estimated. Let SE_X denote whether state X can be securely estimated or not. Then, the following formalization specifies when a state is securely estimated:

$$\forall_Z \ \forall_{X \in StateSet_Z} \ S_Z \rightarrow SE_X$$

$$\forall_X \ SE_X \rightarrow \exists_Z \ S_Z \wedge (X \in StateSet_Z)$$

If $SecUMsr_E$ denotes whether one or more measurements within $UMsrSet_E$ are secured, the following relation is true:

$$\forall_E \ \exists_{Z \in UMsrSet_E} \ SecUMsr_E \rightarrow S_Z$$

Now, the secured observability constraint (*SecuredObservability*) is formalized ensuring that each state/variable is covered by the secure measurements and the minimum number (i.e., at least m) of secure measurements (i.e., equations):

$$SecuredObservability \rightarrow (\forall_X \ SE_X) \wedge (\sum_E SecUMsr_E \geq m)$$

k-Resilient Secured Observability Constraint This constraint verifies whether secured observability is ensured even if k field devices (i.e., IEDs and RTUs) are unavailable. A device can be unavailable because of its failure to communicate with the MTU or the next device toward the MTU, due to its technical failure or remote attacks (e.g., DoS) on it or the path toward the destination. In this constraint modeling, RTU failures are only assumed, although formalizations are similar for the failures of IEDs or others.

In order to model this constraint, it is important to define a parameter for each field device to denote whether that device is unavailable. Let $URtu_R$ be denote whether RTU R is unavailable, and thus the following relation holds:

$$\forall_R \ URtu_R \rightarrow \neg Rtu_R$$

The k-resilient secured observability constraint (*ResilientSecuredObservability*) is formalized as follows:

$$ResilientSecuredObservability \rightarrow \forall_{\sum_R URtu_R \leq k} SecuredObservability$$

The above formalization of the k-resilient secured observability constraint needs to execute all possible combinations of RTU failures up to the number k, which is not efficient. Therefore, an efficient but heuristic-based modeling of this constraint are discussed below.

Let $SRtuMsr_{R,Z}$ denote whether measurement Z is securely transmitted from the IED associated with this measurement to the MTU through RTU R. Then, $SRtuMsr_{R,Z}$ is defined as follows when there is only one intermediate RTU in the transmission path:

$$SRtuMsr_{R,Z} \rightarrow \exists_I (Z \in MsrSet_I) \wedge SecuredDelivery(I, R, M)$$

When, there are two or more intermediate RTUs in this transmission path, the RTU at the top of the hierarchy is the most critical one with respect to the availability of these RTUs. Therefore, this critical RTU needs to be considered in defining $SRtuMsr_{R,Z}$, as shown in the below for two intermediate RTUs:

$$\forall_R \forall_Z \; SRtuMsr_{R,Z} \rightarrow \exists_I (Z \in MsrSet_I) \wedge \exists_{R'} SecuredDelivery(I, R', R, M)$$

Let $SRtuState_{R,X}$ denote whether RTU R securely transmits a measurement that is influenced by state X. Then, the following constraint holds:

$$\forall_R \forall_X \; SRtuState_{R,X} \rightarrow \exists_Z SRtuMsr_{R,Z} \wedge (X \in StateSet_Z)$$

A state can be securely estimated even after k failures of RTUs, considering the worst case when all of these unavailable RTUs are responsible for transmitting different measurements associated with this state, if there is at least one available RTU that also transmits one or more measurements corresponding to that state. Moreover, it is also required to ensure that there are sufficient unique measurements to observe the system. The number of missing unique measurements must be considered when k RTUs are unavailable. The most conservative calculation of this number is taking the maximum possible missing unique measurements for k unavailable RTUs. Since it needs union operations of unique measurement sets for all combinations of k RTUs, a heuristic can be applied to calculate this number by considering the average number of unique measurements that an RTU transmits. However, this heuristic approach cannot ensure the observability. A sound and complete, as well as time efficient, modeling of this constraint remains as a topic for further research. Let $SecUMsrRtu_k$ be the number of missing unique measurements when k RTUs are unavailable. Now, k-resilient secured observability constraint is formalized in the following formula:

$$ResilientSecuredObservability \rightarrow$$

$$\forall_X (\sum_R SRtuState_{R,X} \geq k + 1) \wedge$$

$$((\sum_E SecUMsr_E) - SecUMsrRtu_{E,k} \geq m)$$

Appendix A presents a different approach of formally analyzing SCADA resiliency. Although both of these approaches use formal models, the main distinction between these two is that this approach finds the satisfaction of the resilient observability constraint while the formal model presented in the appendix looks for threat vectors that can fail the resiliency requirement.

Bad Data Detectability Constraint The obtained measurements for observability must be able to detect bad data. Note that a measurement can be secured or trusted, but the data itself can be an outlier due to containing noise (random variations) and other inaccuracies at the censor/meter corresponding to this measurement, or the censor/meter being compromised. If there is a single measurement associated with a state, then the measurement is a critical one and it is not possible to detect if that measurement is bad. Therefore, in order to detect bad data it is required to have at least two measurements corresponding to each state, if it is assumed that no more than one measurement among them can be bad at a time. The bad data detectability constraint can be generalized as k, r-resilient bad data detectability, where if k RTUs (IEDs) are unavailable, the bad data is detectable even if r measurements are available. The detection of the bad data relies on secured measurements, since non-secured measurements cannot be trusted [8]. This constraint is modeled by extending the formalization of the previous constraint, assuming the RTU failures only:

$$ResilientBadDataDetectability \rightarrow \forall_X \left(\sum_R SRtuState_{R,X} \geq k + r + 1 \right)$$

This is the worst case scenario modeling, where an RTU, corresponding to a state, may be involved with transmitting only a single measurement associated with that state.

3.3.3 Implementation

This section briefly discusses the implementation of the model and illustrates the model's execution with an example.

3.3.3.1 SMT Encoding

Similar to the case of implementing AMI security verification model, SMT is used to encode the SCADA security verification model. The solution to the model gives the result *sat* or *unsat*. The *sat* result shows the detailed scenario that makes the constraints or requirements satisfied. For example, in this particular modeling it shows the measurements that are secure (authenticated and integrity protected), as a result of which the observability is secure. In the case of *unsat*, the *unsat-core* can be analyzed to trace the constraint violations, i.e., the potential threat points.

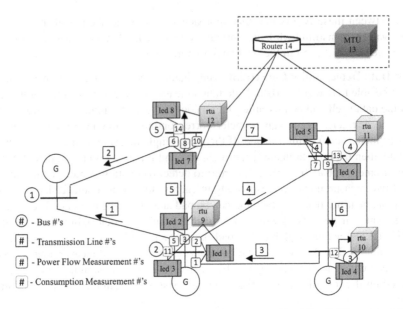

Fig. 3.5 An example SCADA topology of a five-bus power grid. The IEDs, RTUs, and the MTU are numbered in a sequence. The measurements (boxes with round corners) associated with the IEDs are shown using lines

3.3.3.2   An Example

This example demonstrates the k-resilient secured observability constraint. The small five-bus SCADA system considered in this example is shown in Fig. 3.5. The corresponding input is partially presented in Table A.1. The input includes primarily the Jacobian matrix corresponding to the SCADA system, the topology (connectivity between the communicating devices and the association of the measurements with the IEDs), and security profiles of each communicating host pair. In this example, it is assumed that the measurements are taken or collected by different IEDs only and these measurements are sent to an MTU (i.e., the SCADA server at the control center) through RTUs. Each row of the Jacobian matrix corresponds to a measurement (first row corresponds to measurement 1, and so on). Each row has five entries (columns) for each state (corresponding to each bus). The resiliency requirements specify that the secured observability must be satisfied even if an IED or an RTU is unavailable. The solution to the formal model corresponding to this example returns a satisfiable answer, i.e., the given SCADA system is securely observable.

From the assignment to the variables, it is found that all of the measurements, except measurements 1, 2, and 12, are transmitted securely to the MTU, and these measurements are sufficient to observe the system even an IED or an RTU is unavailable. However, if the security properties of the communication from RTU 9 to the MTU is considered as authentication-only (e.g., hmac [7]), then there is no solution even if the security is increased for RTU 10 to both authentication and data integrity protection (rsa and aes [6, 11]). This is because RTU 9 is more critical than RTU 10, as the former node is responsible for transmitting a greater number of measurements than the latter. In this case, if we reduce the resiliency requirement to unavailability of a single IED only, while no unavailability of RTUs, then there is again a satisfiable solution.

3.4 Scalability of the Security Analysis Framework

This section presents some evaluation results that demonstrate the scalability of the security analysis framework in terms of time and memory. These results are generated by evaluating different constraints on synthetic configuration data.

The scalability analysis of the security analysis framework is performed based on the formal model of the security constraint verification. This scalability analysis is also presented according to the AMI-specific framework. Since the number of devices, particularly the smart meters, in an AMI system is much larger than the number of field devices in a SCADA system, these results are sufficient to manifest the scalability of the framework. The size of an AMI system is often referred to the number of meters, which is proportional to the number of collectors. According to the AMI system modeled in this section, the number of collectors depends on the number of zones and their sizes. The evaluation experiments are performed considering 100 and 50 m and collector classes, respectively. Each collector zone consists of around 1000 collectors, while each collector is connected with 10 m (of 2 random meter classes) on average. These experiments are executed on a system with an Intel Core i3 processor and 4 GB memory, and running a 32-bit operating system.

3.4.1 Time Complexity Analysis

Figure 3.6a, b show the impact of the network size on the time for executing the security verification model. The figures show the verification time for different invariant constraints (i.e., reporting mode, collector resource, and reachability) and user-driven constraints (i.e., assured data delivery and availability protection constraint). A significant part of the constraint analysis time is covered by the modeling time, which is almost linearly dependent on the network size that varies with the number of zones. Verifications of some constraints (e.g., reachability) involves all (or a large portion of) possible potential source/target nodes that implicitly increase with the number of zones. Thus, the verification time of such constraints increases more with the size of the network than that of the constraints (e.g., collector resource), which are involved with the class size only. Usually, the

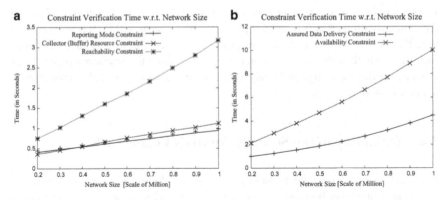

Fig. 3.6 Impact of network size on (**a**) invariant and (**b**) user-driven constraints verification time

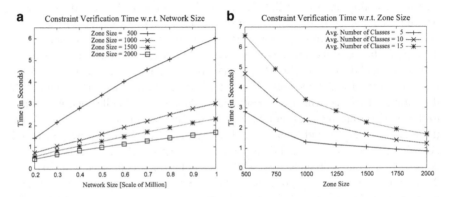

Fig. 3.7 Impact of (**a**) the zone size and (**b**) the number of collector classes per zone on constraint verification time

user-driven constraint analysis time is more than the invariant constraint analysis time (as shown in Fig. 3.6b), since most of the former type of constraints subsume the later type of constraints.

The constraint verification time with respect to the network size is shown in Fig. 3.7a for different network zone sizes. It can easily observe that the analysis time significantly reduces with the increase in the number of collectors in the zone. This reduction becomes more prominent when the network size increases. This is due to the fact that the number of zones decreases as the zone size increases, which in turn decreases the overall model size and the potential sources/targets. Figure 3.7b shows the constraint verification time with respect to the zone size for different numbers of average classes per zone. The figure shows that the time increases if the average number of classes in a zone increases.

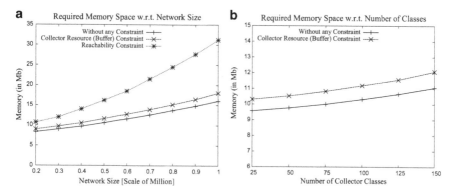

Fig. 3.8 Impact of (**a**) the network size and (**b**) the number of classes on memory requirement

3.4.2 Memory Complexity Analysis

The memory requirement of the SMT solver [14] is evaluated by changing the network size (i.e., number of zones) and the number of classes. Such analysis results are presented in Fig. 3.8a, b which shows almost linear growth of the memory with the network size. Similar to the analysis time, the memory for constraint verification is the sum of the memory for modeling of the AMI configuration and that for modeling a constraint. The figures justify this by showing that less memory is required when no constraint is verified. The constraints involving more quantifiers require larger memory for encoding. Figure 3.8a shows such a comparison between collector resource and reachability constraints.

3.4.3 Time Complexity in Unsatisfied Cases

If the model size increases significantly, the solver may fail to give a solution. An increase of the model size depends not only on the problem size but also on the constraint type. Such events are shown in Fig. 3.9a, b. The figures show the time and memory requirements of verifying the all reachability constraint (*ReachableConstr* for all collectors to the headend system) as well as the cyber bandwidth constraint (*LinkBwConstr*). The modeling of *LinkBwConstr* also requires knowing all the traffics (and traffic size) from collectors to the headend passing through a link at a particular time (according to the reporting schedules). Due to the modeling of all possible traffics between the collectors and the headend, the model size becomes very large. The figures show that if the number of collectors increases more than 23,000 (arrow sign in the figure), the cyber-bandwidth constraint verification fails. Similarly, the reachability satisfaction constraint fails if the number of collectors is over 26,000. These failures happen due to the *out-of-memory-exception* given by

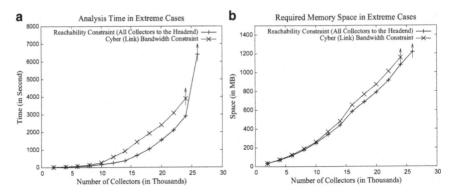

Fig. 3.9 (**a**) Impact of the AMI network size on the analysis time and (**b**) the memory requirement for cyber bandwidth constraint verification. The graphs also show that the analysis of this constraint may fail when the number of collectors increases more than some certain labels

the SMT solver. Figure 3.9b shows the memory consumed by the model. However, the 64 bit implementation of the formal model overcomes this memory explosion problem.

3.5 Summary

Automated analysis of smart grid configurations is an important but challenging problem. A smart grid contains a large number of cyber and physical devices that exhibit highly dependent configuration parameters, which makes potential mis-configurations and security vulnerabilities likely. This chapter presents automated smart grid configuration verification, diagnosis, and repair techniques, particularly for AMI and SCADA, two major components of a smart grid. Various AMI and SCADA specific constraints and requirements are defined and modeled that are essential to protect smart grids from various security threats. According to these constraints, logic-based threat verification models are formalized and efficient SMT-based logics are applied to implement and solve these models. The security analysis framework performs static configuration analysis and determine potential threats as the violations of the smart grid security requirements. The evaluation results show that this framework offers high scalability and this efficiency is achieved by applying the property level abstractions in the model.

References

1. A. Abur, A.G. Exposito, *Power System State Estimation: Theory and Implementation* (CRC Press, New York, 2004)
2. E. Al-Shaer et al., Network configuration in a box: towards end-to-end verification of network reachability and security, in *IEEE International Conference on Network Protocols (ICNP)*, NY (2009), pp. 107–116
3. L. de Moura, N. Bjørner, Z3: an efficient SMT solver, in *International Conference on Tools and Algorithms for the Construction and Analysis of Systems* (2008)
4. Guide to Industrial Control Systems (ICS) Security, NIST Special Publication 800-82 (Revision 1) (2013), http://dx.doi.org/10.6028/NIST.SP.800-82r1
5. IBM Software, Managing big data for smart grids and smart meters (2012), http://www-935.ibm.com/services/multimedia/Managing_big_data_for_smart_grids_and_smart_meters.pdf
6. J. Jonsson, B. Kaliski, *Public-Key Cryptography Standards (PKCS) #1: RSA Cryptography Specifications Version 2.1.* (RFC Editor, USA, 2003)
7. H. Krawczyk, M. Bellare, R. Canetti, *HMAC: Keyed-Hashing for Message Authentication* (RFC Editor, USA, 1997)
8. Y. Liu, P. Ning, M.K. Reiter, False data injection attacks against state estimation in electric power grids, in *ACM Conference on Computer and Communications Security (CCS)*, Chicago, November 2009, pp. 21–32
9. R. Nieuwenhuis, A. Oliveras, On SAT modulo theories and optimization problems, in *Theory and Applications of Satisfiability Testing (SAT)*. Lecture Notes in Computer Science, vol. 4121 (Springer, New York, 2006), pp. 156–169
10. NISTIR 7628: Guidelines for Smart Grid Cyber Security, Smart grid inter-operability panel- cyber security working group (2010), http://www.nist.gov/smartgrid/upload/nistir-7628_total.pdf
11. W. Stallings, The advanced encryption standard. Cryptologia **26**(3), 165–188 (2002). ISSN:0161-1194
12. HP Technical, Using the HP vertica analytics platform to manage massive volumes of smart meter data (2014), http://www.odbms.org/2014/06/hp-vertica-analytics-platform-manage-massive-volumes-smart-meter-data/
13. A.J. Wood, B.F. Wollenberg, *Power Generation, Operation, and Control*, 2nd edn. (Wiley, New York, 1996)
14. The Z3 Theorem Prover, Microsoft Research (2015), https://github.com/Z3Prover/z3/wiki. Accessed 2015

References

Chapter 4
Security Analytics for EMS Modules

In modern energy control centers, the energy management system (EMS) refers to a set of computational tools which are employed for system wide monitoring, analysis, control, and operation. A schematic diagram of EMS and its modules are shown in Fig. 1.6 in Chap. 1. State estimation is the core module in EMS that estimates the system state variables from a set of real-time telemetered measurements (from meters) and topology statuses (from breakers and switches). The term "states" denotes bus voltages, from which power flows through transmission lines can be computed. As seen in Fig. 1.6, the output of state estimation is required by several other modules, i.e., optimal power flow (OPF), contingency analysis, and automatic generation control (AGC), for economic dispatch calculations and security assessment.

Cyber technologies are increasingly used in smart power grids with the promise of providing larger capacity, higher efficiency, and more reliability [8]. While this integration helps energy providers to offer smarter services, real time demand responses, and economic advantages, power grids also become vulnerable to cyber attacks. Particularly, cyber intrusions and false data injections can be launched against power grids, which can cause improper controls leading to serious damages, including power outages and destruction of critical equipment [11, 13].

In the case of state estimation, an attacker can compromise meters or communication media to introduce malicious measurements, which can lead to incorrect state estimation. There are bad data detection algorithms [1, 14], which detect bad measurements principally based on the square of differences between observed and estimated measurements with some threshold values. It has been shown that an attacker can generate bad measurements with the knowledge of the grid, which can bypass the bad data detection [12]. As a result, states are estimated incorrectly, which can easily lead the system to a non-optimal and vulnerable situation. Stealthy attacks of this kind are known as undetected false data injection (UFDI) attacks. It is

© Springer International Publishing Switzerland 2016
E. Al-Shaer, M.A. Rahman, *Security and Resiliency Analytics for Smart Grids*,
Advances in Information Security 67, DOI 10.1007/978-3-319-32871-3_4

crucial to develop a threat analytics framework which can identify potential stealthy attacks considering different attack models, as well as the interdependency among different EMS modules.

This chapter presents a formal framework for verifying stealthy attacks and their impact on state estimation. This framework models these stealthy attacks considering a comprehensive list of attack attributes that can flexibly represent an adversary, and thus it allows a grid operator to analyze and explore potential threats under different attack scenarios. The framework also models the impact of UFDI attacks on other interdependent modules, particularly OPF, to understand the economic loss.

This chapter also presents two mechanisms to protect the state estimation against stealthy attacks. The first mechanism is an automated technique that considers the adversary's capability and the grid operator's resource limitation, and accordingly synthesizes a security architecture. This security architecture specifies a set of measurements or buses that need to be secured, to make false data injection attacks detectable. The second mechanism provides proactive security to the grid by introducing agility in the system with the help of moving target defense strategies.

4.1 Preliminaries

This section includes the preliminaries that are building block of the security analytics framework presented in this chapter.

4.1.1 DC Power Flow Mode

The DC power flow model, which has been widely used to analyze stealthy attacks on state estimation (e.g., [12, 21]). Although the DC model is simplistic, it is useful in preliminary analytical power systems studies. In this model, the power balance equations are described in terms of a lossless power system [23]. With voltage magnitudes at all buses fixed at 1 per unit (p.u.), the only variables are phase angles. Therefore, the voltage phasor at bus i is given by $1\angle\theta_i$. Denoting the admittance of the transmission line between buses i and j by Y_{ij}, the real power flow (P_{ij}) across a transmission line is given by: $P_{ij} = Y_{ij}(\theta_i - \theta_j)$ where Y_{ij} is the reciprocal of the reactance. The model expresses the power-balance constraint which equates the algebraic sum of powers incident at every bus to zero. This yields a linear system of equations of the form: $[\mathbf{B}][\boldsymbol{\theta}] = [\mathbf{P}]$. One of the buses is designated as the reference bus (also known as the slack bus), where $\theta_i = 0$. Assuming n buses, $[\mathbf{B}]$ is an $n - 1$ dimensional square matrix, and $\mathbf{P}$ is an $n - 1$ dimensional column vector whose elements denote the net power demand (i.e., load minus generation) at a bus and $[\boldsymbol{\theta}]$ is a column vector of unknown phases corresponding to the bus voltage phasors. The model solves unknown bus voltages, given admittances of the lines and net power demands at the buses. This linear model provides the basis for DC state estimation*DC state estimation* which is described next.

4.1.2   State Estimation

The state estimation problem based on the DC model is to estimate the bus voltages given several measurements of transmission line power flows. Specifically, one needs to estimate n number of the state variables $\mathbf{x} = (x_1, x_2, \cdots, x_n)^T$ based on m number of meter measurements $\mathbf{z} = (z_1, z_2, \cdots, z_m)^T$ [1]. Under the DC power flow assumptions, the measurement model is linear (i.e., the measured power flows are linear functions of the bus voltages) and hence the measurement model reduces to:

$$\mathbf{z} = \mathbf{H}\mathbf{x} + \mathbf{e}, \text{ where } \mathbf{H} = (h_{i,j})_{m \times n}$$

$\mathbf{H}$ is known as Jacobian matrix. The measurement set has redundant elements (i.e., $m > n$), which are used for creating an over-determined set of linear equations. The redundancy enables the detection, elimination, and smoothing of unavoidable gross measurement errors. When the measurement error distribution is Gaussian with zero mean, state estimate $\hat{\mathbf{x}}$ is expressed by the following equation:

$$\hat{\mathbf{x}} = (\mathbf{H}^T \mathbf{W} \mathbf{H})^{-1} \mathbf{H}^T \mathbf{W} \mathbf{z} \tag{4.1}$$

Here, $\mathbf{W}$ is a diagonal "weighting" matrix whose elements are reciprocals of meter error variances. Thus, estimated measurements are calculated as $\mathbf{H}\hat{\mathbf{x}}$. The measurement residual $\|\mathbf{z} - \mathbf{H}\hat{\mathbf{x}}\|$ is used to determine bad data. If $\|\mathbf{z} - \mathbf{H}\hat{\mathbf{x}}\|$ is greater than τ, a selected threshold value, it indicates bad data.

4.1.3   Topology Processor

EMS uses a *topology processor* (refer to Fig. 1.6) to map the grid topology. This processor receives telemetered statuses of various switches and circuit breakers in the system to determine network connectivity. When the connectivity matrix $\mathbf{A}$ and the branch admittance matrix $\mathbf{D}$ are known, the measurement matrix $\mathbf{H}$ is computed as follows (as in [19]):

$$\mathbf{H} = \begin{bmatrix} \mathbf{DA} \\ -\mathbf{DA} \\ \mathbf{A}^T \mathbf{DA} \end{bmatrix} \tag{4.2}$$

Matrices **DA** (i.e., multiplication of **D** and **A**) and −**DA** represent the line power flows in forward and backward directions, respectively. The matrix $\mathbf{A}^T\mathbf{DA}$ represents power consumption at the buses.

4.1.4   Optimal Power Flow

The state estimated solution (from Eq. (4.1)) estimates bus voltages from which the system power flows are computed. Summing up the net power flows incident on a bus then yields the estimated power (or load) at that bus. System conditions determined from state estimation are then used in the OPF module. The OPF problem aims to minimize the total cost of *generation* subject to the following constraints: (1) the total system load is served and (2) equipment ratings, transmission line limits, and control variables are satisfied [23]. Denoting the generation cost of generator k by $C_k(P_k)$, where C_k depends on the nature of the plant (e.g., fossil fired, combined cycle, etc.), the OPF routine with respect to the DC power flow model is described by:

$$min \sum_i C_k(P_k) \text{ s.t.} \tag{4.3}$$

$$[\mathbf{B}][\theta] = [\mathbf{P}] \tag{4.4}$$

$$|P_{ij}| \leq P_{ij}^{max} \tag{4.5}$$

$$P_k^{min} \leq P_k \leq P_k^{max} \tag{4.6}$$

Here, Eq. (4.3) describes the objective function of minimizing the total cost of generation, subject to power flow constraints in Eq. (4.4), transmission line capacities in Eq. (4.5), and generation capacities in Eq. (4.6).

4.1.5   UFDI Attack

Liu et al. have introduced a interesting kind of attack, named UFDI attack, against state estimation [12]. They have shown that it is possible to generate a stealthy attack vector that can bypass the bad data detection process. The idea is briefly explained here. Consider an attacker who injects arbitrary false data **a** to the original measurements **z** such that $\mathbf{a} = \mathbf{Hc}$, i.e., a linear combination of the column vectors of **H**. Here, **c** is added to the original state estimate $\hat{\mathbf{x}}$ due to the injection of **a**. Since $\mathbf{z} + \mathbf{a} = \mathbf{H}(\hat{\mathbf{x}} + \mathbf{c})$, the residual $||(\mathbf{z} + \mathbf{a}) - \mathbf{H}(\hat{\mathbf{x}} + \mathbf{c})||$ still remains the same as $||\mathbf{z} - \mathbf{H}\hat{\mathbf{x}}||$. Thus, the bad data detection is evaded. Note that this requires knowledge of **H**, i.e., the system topology, electrical properties of the transmission lines, and measurement configurations. Moreover, the attacker's capability should be considered to identify the potential threats on state estimation.

4.1.6 Attack Attributes

In order to describe attacks in their most general form it is crucial to model adversarial capabilities characterized in terms of different attributes, which mainly include the adversary's access capability, resources, and knowledge of the system. The four attack attributes considered in this framework are as follows:

- **Accessibility:** An attacker may not have access to all of the measurements when physical or remote access to substations is restricted, or when certain measurements are already secured. For example, in order to inject false data into the measurements taken at a substation (i.e., bus), an attacker needs to have the access to that substation (or to the corresponding remote terminal unit) [22].
- **Resource Constraint:** An adversary may be constrained in cost or effort to mount attacks on vastly distributed measurements. In such cases, an adversary is constrained to compromising or altering a limited subset of measurements at a time. It is useful to represent this resource limitation with respect to buses. In order to launch an attack, if it requires false data injections to a set of measurements distributed in many substations (i.e., buses), then it would be harder for the attacker to inject false data into those measurements compared to the set of measurements distributed in a small number of substations.
- **Grid Topology and Knowledge:** State estimation of a power system is done based on the given topology (i.e., connectivity among the buses) of the grid. This topology is mapped by the topology processor. For a successful UFDI attack, an attacker needs to know the grid topology and the electrical parameters of the transmission lines, which is not trivial [12]. In the case of partial knowledge, the attacker's capabilities become restricted. On the other hand, an attacker can inflict novel UFDI attacks against state estimation by conveying false status information at the transmitting devices or media, such that the topology generated by the processor includes one or more open lines (i.e., non-existing in the true topology), or excludes one or more closed lines (i.e., existing in the true topology).
- **Attack Target:** An attacker may have the aim of corrupting a chosen set of states or a specific portion of the system, which often requires to perform false data injections to a certain set of measurements.

Modeling the state estimation, its interdependency with other EMS modules, and the consideration of all these attack attributes in a single model are crucial to identify potential stealthy threats and their impact on the power grid.

4.2   Stealthy Attack Verification

This section presents the model of verifying the potentiality of UFDI attacks. This verification utilizes a number of parameters that denote different system properties and attack attributes. Although these parameters are introduced below, some of them are presented in Table 4.1 for a quick reference.

4.2.1   Formalizations of Power Flow Equations

According to the DC power flow model, the admittance of a line or branch is computed from its reactance. The direction of the line is taken based on the current flow direction, i.e., from one end-bus to another end-bus. The two end-buses of line i are denoted using f_i (*from-bus*) and e_i (*to-bus*), where $1 \leq i \leq l$, $1 \leq f_i, e_i \leq b$, and b is the number of buses. The admittance of the line is denoted by d_i.

Table 4.1 Modeling parameters

Notation	Definition
b	The number of buses in the grid.
l	The number of lines in the grid topology.
f_i	The *from-bus* of line i.
e_i	The *to-bus* of line i.
d_i	The admittance of line i.
g_i	Whether the admittance of line i is known.
P_i^L	The power flow through line i.
P_j^B	The power consumption at bus j.
θ_j	The state value, i.e., the voltage phase angle, at bus j.
n	The number of states.
m	The number of potential measurements.
a_i	Whether measurement i is required to be altered for the attack.
c_j	Whether state j is infected/affected due to false data injection.
h_j	Whether any measurement residing at bus j is required to be changed.
t_i	Whether potential measurement i is taken (i.e., reported by a meter).
r_i	Whether measurement i is accessible to the attacker.
s_i	Whether the measurement is secured or not.
u_i	Whether line i exists in the true (real) topology.
v_i	Whether line i is fixed in the topology.
w_i	Whether the status information regarding line i is secured.
p_i	Whether line i is excluded from the topology by an exclusion attack.
q_i	Whether line i is included in the topology by an inclusion attack.
k_i	Whether line i is considered (though it may not exist) in the topology.

Each row of $\mathbf{H}$ corresponds to a power equation. The first l rows correspond to the forward line power flow measurements. The next l rows are the backward line power flow measurements, which are the same as the first l except the directions of the power flows are opposite. Let P_i^L denotes the power flow through line i, while P_j^B denotes the power consumption at bus j, and θ_j denote the state value (i.e., the voltage phase angle at bus j). Then, the following relation holds between the power flow of line i (P_i^L) and the states of the connected buses (f_i and e_i):

$$\forall_{1 \leq i \leq l} \ P_i^L = d_i(\theta_{f_i} - \theta_{e_i}) \tag{4.7}$$

Equation (4.7) specifies that power flow P_i^L depends on the difference of the connected buses' phase angles and the line admittance. The last b rows of $\mathbf{H}$ correspond to the bus power consumptions. The power consumption at bus j is simply the summation of the power flows of the lines connected to this bus. Let $\mathbb{L}_{j,in}$ and $\mathbb{L}_{j,out}$ be the sets of incoming and outgoing lines of bus j, respectively. Then, the following equation represents the power consumption at bus j:

$$\forall_{1 \leq j \leq b} \ P_j^B = \sum_{i \in \mathbb{L}_{j,in}} P_i^L - \sum_{i \in \mathbb{L}_{j,out}} P_i^L \tag{4.8}$$

The power consumption at a bus is also equal to the load power at this bus minus the power injected to it by the connected generators. If P_j^D and P_j^G denote the load power and generated power of bus j, respectively, the following equation holds:

$$\forall_{1 \leq j \leq b} \ P_j^B = P_j^D - P_j^G \tag{4.9}$$

If bus j is not connected with any generator, then $P_j^G = 0$. Similarly, if bus j does not have any load, then $P_j^D = 0$. Basically, state estimation in DC model is the solution to the linear equations for all of the measurements (P_i^Ls and P_j^Bs) given the line admittances (d_is).

In the DC model, two measurements, the forward and backward power flows, can be taken for each line. The term "taken" is used here to specify that the measurement is recorded by a meter or censor at a targeted point (i.e., one end of the transmission line), and it is reported to the control center. For each bus, a measurement can be taken for the power consumption at the bus. Therefore, for a power system with l number of lines and b number of buses, there are $2l + b$ number of potential measurements (z_is). Though a significantly smaller number of measurements are sufficient for state estimation, redundancy is provided to identify and filter bad data. Parameter t_i denotes whether potential measurement z_i is taken. Note that though m is often used to represent the taken measurements, in this model, m represents the maximum number of potential measurements (i.e., $2l + b$).

4.2.2   Formalization of Change in State Estimation

Parameter c_j denotes whether state x_j $(1 \leq j \leq n)$ is affected (i.e., changed to an incorrect value) due to false data injection. In the DC model, each state corresponds to a bus. Thus, n is equal to b. The attack on state x_j specifies that the phase angle at bus j is changed. This condition is formalized as follows:

$$\forall_{1 \leq j \leq n} \ c_j \rightarrow (\Delta\theta_j \neq 0) \tag{4.10}$$

From Eq. (4.7), it is obvious that a change of P_i^L is required based on the changes in state x_{f_i} (θ_{f_i}) and/or state x_{e_i} (θ_{e_i}). In the case of false data injection, P_i^L, θ_{f_i}, and θ_{e_i} are changed to P'^L_i, θ'_{f_i}, and θ'_{e_i}, respectively, and Eq. (4.7) turns into the following form:

$$P'^L_i = d_i(\theta'_{f_i} - \theta'_{e_i})$$

The subtraction of Eq. (4.7) from the above equation represents whether there are changes in the measurements and the states. The following is the resultant equation:

$$\Delta P_i^L = d_i(\Delta\theta_{f_i} - \Delta\theta_{e_i})$$

In this equation, $\Delta P_i^L = P'^L_i - P_i^L$, $\Delta\theta_{f_i} = \theta'_{f_i} - \theta_{f_i}$, and $\Delta\theta_{e_i} = \theta'_{e_i} - \theta_{e_i}$. If $\Delta\theta_{f_i} \neq 0$ (or $\Delta\theta_{e_i} \neq 0$), then it is obvious that state x_{f_i} (or x_{e_i}) is changed (i.e., attacked). The above relation for line i holds only if the line is closed which is determined by the topology processor from the breaker and switch statuses. Parameter k_i represents whether line i exists in the topology. This constraint is formalized as follows:

$$\forall_{1 \leq i \leq l} \ k_i \rightarrow (\Delta P_i^L = d_i(\Delta\theta_{f_i} - \Delta\theta_{e_i})) \tag{4.11}$$

If a line is not considered in the topology, then there should be no requirement of false data injection to corresponding measurements for launching UFDI attacks:

$$\forall_{1 \leq i \leq l} \ \neg k_i \rightarrow (\Delta P_i^L = 0) \tag{4.12}$$

4.2.3   Formalization of Topology Change

The topology of a power grid represents the connectivity among the grid buses. An attacker can inject false data in the topology information sent by various circuit breakers and switches in order to change the topology. Changes in the topology assumed in this model include: (1) exclusion of a closed line from the topology (*exclusion attack*), and (2) inclusion of an open line in the topology (*inclusion attack*). It is also assumed that the adversary coordinates a topology error with other measurements to render the attack undetected. Therefore, a UFDI attack can be performed by leveraging the modified topology.

Some of the transmission lines in the topology always remain closed, i.e., either they are never opened or there is no way to open them. These lines form the core of the topology. The switch or breaker status can be secured and thus the lines associated with them are always faithfully represented in state estimation. In order to model all these properties plus the topology change, the following parameters are used. Parameter u_i denotes whether line i is the true or real topology, while v_i and w_i denote whether the line is fixed and the line status is secure, respectively. In order to denote exclusion and inclusion attacks on line i, parameters p_i and q_i are used, respectively.

In the case of an inclusion attack, a line is considered in the topology though the line is open in reality. Conversely, a closed line in service is omitted in an exclusion attack. These are formalized as follows:

$$\forall_{1 \le i \le l} \ k_i \rightarrow (u_i \wedge \neg p_i) \vee (\neg u_i \wedge q_i) \tag{4.13}$$

A line can be excluded from the topology if and only if the line exists in the real or true topology and it is not a securely fixed line. This is formalized as follows:

$$\forall_{1 \le i \le l} \ p_i \rightarrow u_i \wedge \neg fl_i \wedge \neg w_i \tag{4.14}$$

Similarly, a line can be included in the topology if the following condition holds:

$$\forall_{1 \le i \le l} \ q_i \rightarrow \neg u_i \wedge \neg w_i \tag{4.15}$$

Note that for a topology error to remain undetected, it is necessary to alter certain measurements in necessary amounts. If a closed line is excluded from the topology, the corresponding line power flow measurement must be zero. As the states remain the same after the topology change, the corresponding connected buses' power consumption measurements are adjusted accordingly. On the other hand, when an open line is included in the topology, there should be a non-zero line power flow according to the phase difference between the connected buses. Let $\Delta \bar{P}_i^L$ be the change amount in the power flow measurement of line i in the case of a topology change. Then, the following constraints hold:

$$\forall_{1 \le i \le l} \ p_i \rightarrow (\Delta \bar{P}_i^L = -P_i^L) \tag{4.16}$$

$$\forall_{1 \le i \le l} \ q_i \rightarrow (\Delta \bar{P}_i^L = P_i^L) \tag{4.17}$$

If no exclusion or inclusion attack is done on line i, then $\Delta \bar{P}_i^L = 0$. Now, if line power flow measurement i (or $l + i$) needs to change, according to Eqs. (4.16) and (4.17), the adversary needs to know P_i^L. In the case of an exclusion attack, P_i^L already exists (i.e., the actual measurement) and the attacker must have access to it. In the case of an inclusion attack, P_i^L needs to be estimated based on the difference between the states of the connecting buses.

4.2.4   Formalization of False Data Injection to Measurements

To launch an stealthy attack, the adversary must know the required changes to be applied to the measurements for coordinating the attack. The required change for a power flow measurement is the summation of individual changes that are required for topology poisoning and state corruption. If $\Delta P^L_{i,total}$ is the total change required on the line i's power flow, then:

$$\forall_{1 \leq i \leq l} \; \Delta P^L_{i,total} = \Delta P^L_i + \Delta \bar{P}^L_i \tag{4.18}$$

According to Eq. (4.8), the change in the measurement of the power consumption $(\Delta P^B_{j,total})$ at a bus depends on the total changes done in the power flow measurements of the lines incident to this bus. Therefore,

$$\forall_{1 \leq j \leq b} \; \Delta P^B_{j,total} = \sum_{i \in \mathbb{L}_{j,in}} \Delta P^L_{i,total} - \sum_{i \in \mathbb{L}_{j,out}} \Delta P^L_{i,total} \tag{4.19}$$

Parameter a_i denotes whether measurement z_i $(1 \leq i \leq m)$ is required to be altered (by injecting false data) for the attack. If any measurement at bus j is required to be changed, h_j becomes true.

When $\Delta P^L_{i,total} \neq 0$, the measurements corresponding to line i (i.e., t_i and t_{l+i}) are required to be altered if they are taken. Similarly, when $\Delta P^B_{j,total} \neq 0$, the power consumption measurement at bus j needs to be changed if this measurement is taken. Therefore:

$$\forall_{1 \leq i \leq l} (\Delta P^L_{i,total} \neq 0) \to (t_i \to a_i) \land (t_{l+i} \to a_{l+i})$$
$$\forall_{1 \leq j \leq b} \; (\Delta P^B_{j,total} \neq 0) \to (t_{2l+j} \to a_{2l+j}) \tag{4.20}$$

Conversely, measurement z_i is altered only if it is taken and the corresponding power measurement is changed:

$$\forall_{1 \leq i \leq l} \; a_i \to t_i \land (\Delta P^L_{i,total} \neq 0)$$
$$\forall_{1 \leq i \leq l} \; a_{l+i} \to t_{l+i} \land (\Delta P^L_{i,total} \neq 0) \tag{4.21}$$
$$\forall_{1 \leq j \leq b} \; a_{2l+j} \to t_{2l+j} \land (\Delta P^B_{j,total} \neq 0)$$

4.2.5   Formalization of Attack Attributes

4.2.5.1   Attacker's Knowledge

Although the attacker may not know some of the transmission lines if they exists or not, in this framework the incomplete information is modeled with respect to line admittance only. It is worth mentioning that if the end-buses of a line are unknown, the corresponding row in **A** is fully unknown to the attacker. In this case, there is no way for an adversary to launch UFDI attacks on the system. Parameter g_i is used to denote whether the attacker knows the admittance of line i. When the admittance of a line is unknown, an adversary cannot determine the necessary changes that need to be applied to the measurements associated with that line. This condition is formalized as follows:

$$\forall_{1 \leq i \leq l} \ (\Delta P_i^L \neq 0) \rightarrow ((t_i \vee t_{l+i} \vee t_{f_i} \vee t_{e_i}) \rightarrow g_i) \tag{4.22}$$

The following equation shows an example of specifying the attacker's knowledge about the admittances of the lines:

$$g_1 \wedge g_2 \wedge g_3 \wedge \neg g_4 \wedge \cdots \wedge g_l \tag{4.23}$$

4.2.5.2 Attacker's Accessibility

The attacker usually does not have the necessary physical or remote access to inject false data into all the measurements. Parameter r_i denotes whether measurement z_i is accessible to the attacker. If a measurement is secured, then, although the attacker may have the ability to perform false data injection to the measurement, the false data injection will not be successful. Parameter s_i denotes if the measurement is secured. Hence, the attacker will only be able to change measurement z_i if the following condition holds:

$$\forall_{1 \leq i \leq m} \ a_i \rightarrow r_i \wedge \neg s_i \tag{4.24}$$

It is necessary to specify whether a measurement is secured or not, as well as whether or not a measurement is accessible to the attacker. The following equations are examples of such specifications:

$$\neg s_1 \wedge s_2 \wedge \neg s_3 \wedge \neg s_4 \wedge \cdots \wedge s_m \tag{4.25}$$

$$r_1 \wedge \neg r_2 \wedge r_3 \wedge \neg r_4 \wedge \cdots \wedge r_m \tag{4.26}$$

4.2.5.3 Attacker's Resource

The resource limitation specifies that, at a particular time, the attacker can inject false data into T_A number of measurements, at the maximum:

$$\sum_{1 \leq i \leq l} a_i \leq T_A \tag{4.27}$$

This is the attacker's capability to do simultaneous false data injection.

Due to limited resources, an attacker can only access or compromise a limited number of buses at a particular time. A bus is required to be accessed or compromised if a measurement residing at this bus is required to be altered. Therefore:

$$\forall_{1 \le i \le l} \ a_i \rightarrow h_{f_i}$$
$$\forall_{1 \le i \le l} \ a_{l+i} \rightarrow h_{e_i} \qquad (4.28)$$
$$\forall_{1 \le j \le b} \ a_{2l+j} \rightarrow h_j$$

Let T_H be the maximum number of substations that the attacker can compromise. Then:

$$\sum_{1 \le j \le b} h_j \le T_H \qquad (4.29)$$

4.2.5.4   Attack Target

The attacker most often has a selected set of states for launching an attack. However, the attacker usually has no specification on the rest of the states. Thus, an unspecified state might be attacked or not. For example, if the attacker targets states 1, 4, and 6, then:

$$c_1 \wedge c_4 \wedge c_6 \qquad (4.30)$$

It is possible to launch a UFDI attack on a number of measurements if the attacker can form a cut that divides the grid into two disjoint islands [17]. The attacker can attack all of the buses of one side of the cut with respect to the other side by altering the power flow and consumption measurements of the lines and the buses on the cut. However, in this case, all of the attacked buses have the same change of their states (i.e., phase angles). If the state change of a bus is the same as that of the neighboring buses, then there is no state change relative to each other. In this case, the impact due to the attack might not be significant. Therefore, it is also meaningful to consider the constraints specifying whether state changes are required to be different. For example, if the attacker requires that state 1 and state 4 must have a different amount of change, then:

$$(\theta_1 \ne \theta_4) \wedge \cdots \qquad (4.31)$$

4.2.6   An Example Case Study

This section briefly discusses about the implementation of the formal model and demonstrates it using a synthetic case study.

4.2.6.1 Implementation

The formalizations presented above are encoded into SMT logics [6]. In this encoding, mainly Boolean (i.e., for logical constraints) and real (e.g., for the relation between power flows or consumptions with states) terms are used. The system configurations and the constraints are taken from an input file and a program leveraging the Z3 Dot Net API [24] is developed to parse the input file and encode the formal model. The execution of the model in Z3 provides a verification result, either satisfiable (*sat*) or unsatisfiable (*unsat*). If the result is *unsat*, it means that there is no attack vector that satisfies the constraints. In the case of *sat*, the attack vector is found from the assignments of the variables, a_is, h_js, p_is, and q_is, which represent the measurements (or buses) and topology statuses that must be altered for the attack.

4.2.6.2 Example

This example is based on the IEEE 14-bus test system (see Fig. 4.1) [16]. The input about the line information is shown (partially) in Table 4.2. The line information includes a set of data for each line: line number, end buses of the line, a value indicating the line admittance, the knowledge status (i.e., whether the line admittance is known to the attacker), and three types of data about this line regarding the grid topology (i.e., whether this line is included in the actual topology, whether its existence is fixed in the topology, and whether associated topology information is secured). In this example, the admittances of lines 3, 7, and 17 are unknown. All of the 20 lines (as shown in Fig. 4.1) are included in the true topology, though lines 5 and 13 are not a part of the core topology. The topology statuses regarding these two lines are crucial to estimate whether they are in open state or closed state.

The input about the measurements is partially shown in Table 4.3. Since this system has 14 buses and 20 lines, the maximum number of potential measurements is 54. Each row of Table 4.3 includes (1) whether the measurement is taken for state estimation (all the potential measurements are taken except measurements 5, 10, 14, 19, 22, 27, 30, 35, 43, and 52), (2) whether the measurement is secured (measurements 1, 2, 6, 15, 25, 32, and 41 are secured) and (3) whether the attacker has the accessibility to alter the measurement (e.g., among the taken measurements 1, 2, 3, and 4, measurements 3 and 4 are accessible, while measurements 1 and 2 are inaccessible).

Let the attacker's objective be to attack states 9 and 10 but in different amounts. Due to resource limitations, the attacker cannot alter more than 16 measurements at a time, and these measurements cannot be distributed in more than 7 substations (i.e., buses). The execution of the model corresponding to this example returns *sat* along with the assignments to different variables of the model. According to the assignments, the measurements selected for attacking states 9 and 10 are 8, 9, 16, 18, 20, 28, 29, 36, 38, 40, 44, 47, 50, 51, 53, and 54. These measurements are distributed in buses 4, 7, 9, 10, 11, 13, and 14. If the attacker's resources are

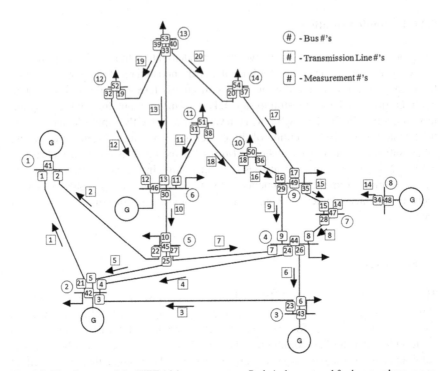

Fig. 4.1 The diagram of the IEEE 14-bus test system. *Red circles* are used for bus numbers, *green squares* are for transmission line numbers, and round cornered *blue squares* are for measurement numbers.

more limited (e.g., 15 measurements and/or 6 buses only), then *unsat* is returned. However, if the attacks on states 9 and 10 can be the same, then there is a solution. In this case, the measurements for false data injection are 8, 9, 11, 13, 28, 29, 31, 33, 39, 44, 46, 47, 49, 51, and 53, while the corresponding buses are 4, 6, 7, 9, 11, and 13. In both of these cases, along with 9 and 10, some other states are also required to be corrupted; only states 9 and 10 cannot be attacked alone.

When the attacker's objective is to attack state 12 only (i.e., no other states will be affected), the execution of the corresponding model shows that measurements 12, 32, 39, 46, and 53 need to be altered. If measurement 46 is considered as secured, then no attack vector is possible in this case. However, if the attacker has the ability to alter the topology information, there is a solution, where line 13 is excluded from the topology by injecting false data into the topology information. In this case, the measurements for false data injection are 12, 13, 32, 33, 39, and 53, which include necessary changes required for the state change along with the topology change.

Table 4.2 Line information of the example in Sect. 4.2.6

Line #	From bus	To bus	Line admittance	Knowledge?	True?	Core?	Secured?	Can alter?
1	1	2	16.90	1	1	1	0	0
2	1	5	4.48	1	1	1	0	0
3	2	3	5.05	0[a]	1	1	0	0
4	2	4	5.67	1	1	1	0	0
5	2	5	5.75	1	1	0[b]	0	0
6	3	4	5.85	1	1	1	0	0
7	4	5	23.75	0	1	1	0	0
8	4	7	4.78	1	1	1	0	0
9	4	9	1.80	1	1	1	0	0
10	5	6	3.97	1	1	1	0	0
11	6	11	5.03	1	1	1	0	0
12	6	12	3.91	1	1	1	0	0
13	6	13	7.68	1	1	0	0	0
14	7	8	5.68	1	1	1	0	0
15	7	9	9.09	1	1	1	0	0
16	9	10	11.83	0	1	1	0	0
17	9	14	3.70	1	1	1	0	0
18	10	11	5.21	1	1	1	0	0
19	12	13	5.00	1	1	1	0	0
20	13	14	2.87	1	1	1	0	0

[a]The attacker does not know the impedance of this line
[b]This line is not fixed in the topology (i.e., it is not a part of the core topology)

Table 4.3 Measurement info of the example in Sect. 4.2.6

Measurement #	Is recorded?	Secured	Can alter?
1	1[a]	1[b]	0
2	1	1	0
3	1	0	1[c]
4	1	0	1
5	0	0	0
...	...	...	...
11	1	0	1
12	1	0	1
13	1	0	1
14	0	0	0
15	1	1	1
...	...	...	...
21	1	0	1
22	0	0	0
23	1	0	1
24	1	0	1
25	1	1	1
...	...	...	...
41	1	1	0
42	1	0	1
43	1	0	1
44	1	0	1
45	1	1	0
...	...	...	...

[a]The measurement is taken or recorded for state estimation
[b]The measurement is secured, especially in terms of integrity
[c]The attacker has the accessibility to alter the measurement

4.3 Impact Analysis of Stealthy Attacks

This section discusses the framework for verifying the impact of stealthy attacks on OPF.

4.3.1 Impact Analysis Framework Design

Figure 4.2 presents the framework design for verifying the impact of stealthy attacks on OPF. The architecture includes two models: (1) the stealthy attack model that finds attack vectors corresponding to stealthy topology attacks, and (2) the OPF

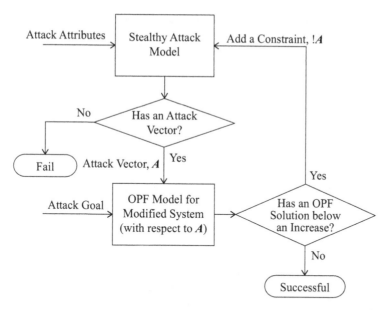

Fig. 4.2 The framework design for analyzing the impact of UFDI attacks on OPF

model that verifies whether there is an OPF solution within a threshold cost. Since the objective is to launch a stealthy attack such that the cost of power generation (according to the OPF solution) increases by a specific amount or more, the idea of impact analysis is as follows. First, the framework looks for an attack vector according to the attack model (i.e., attack attributes). If the attack model gives an attack vector, the system is updated with respect to that vector (i.e., according to the changed loads and the modified topology). Then, the framework verifies whether there is an increase in the generation cost by executing the OPF model. In order to verify this increase, the threshold cost is elevated by adding the expected raise with the original (i.e., in the no attack scenario) OPF solution and then checking whether there is still an OPF solution within this threshold value. If the result is no, then an attack vector is successfully found that can cause a minimum amount of increase in the generation cost. Otherwise, the same process will be executed for a new attack vector until either there is a vector satisfying the objective or there is no more vector. It is worth mentioning that the objective is to increase the generation cost while ensuring convergence of OPF, considering the power generation limit of each generator and the capacity of each transmission line. The framework combines the stealthy attack model and the OPF model into a single model, although they can be executed separately.

The modeling of the impact of stealthy attacks on OPF has two parts: (1) the OPF process as a problem of verifying whether there is a generation dispatch plan satisfying the demand within a threshold generation cost and (2) the feasibility of a stealthy attack inducing a particular increase in the generation cost.

4.3.2   Formalization of Optimal Power Flow

The objective of the OPF is to optimally control the generation according to the load requirement. Let $\hat{P}_j^G$ be the changed power produced by the generator connected at bus j after considering the state estimation result. The main constraint for OPF is that the total generation must be equal to the total expected load. Therefore:

$$\sum_{1 \leq j \leq b} \hat{P}_j^G = \sum_{1 \leq j \leq b} \hat{P}_j^D \tag{4.32}$$

Each generator has lower and upper bounds on power production. If $\hat{P}_{j,max}^G$ and $\hat{P}_{j,min}^G$ denote the maximum and minimum generation limits of the generator at bus j, then this constraint is formalized as follows:

$$\forall_{1 \leq j \leq b} \ \hat{P}_{j,min}^G \leq \hat{P}_j^G \leq \hat{P}_{j,max}^G \tag{4.33}$$

The OPF process considers the entire set of power flow equations as constraints, as illustrated in Eq. (4.4) (Sect. 4.1). In the case of OPF, let $\hat{\theta}$, $\hat{P}_i^L$, and $\hat{P}_j^B$ be the state of bus j, the power flow on line i, and the power consumption at bus j, respectively. Then, in the case of a power flow measurement, the following equation, similar to Eq. (4.7), must hold when the line is considered in the topology:

$$\forall_{1 \leq i \leq l} \ k_i \rightarrow (\hat{P}_i^L = d_i(\hat{\theta}_{f_i} - \hat{\theta}_{e_i})) \tag{4.34}$$

Consequently, the following equations, similar to Eqs. (4.8) and (4.9), must hold:

$$\forall_{1 \leq j \leq b} \ \hat{P}_j^B = \sum_{i \in \mathbb{L}_{j,in}} \hat{P}_i^L - \sum_{i \in \mathbb{L}_{j,out}} \hat{P}_i^L$$
$$\forall_{1 \leq j \leq b} \ \hat{P}_j^B = \hat{P}_j^D - \hat{P}_j^G \tag{4.35}$$

Each line has a capacity for the power flow (i.e., the maximum power that can flow through that line). Let $P_{i,max}^L$ be the upper bound for the line capacity. Therefore:

$$\forall_{1 \leq i \leq l} \ \hat{P}_i^L \leq P_{i,max}^L \tag{4.36}$$

Let $\mathscr{C}_j(.)$ denote the cost function for the generator connected at bus j, which takes the total generated power as the parameter and returns the total cost to generate that power. Usually, $\mathscr{C}_j(.)$ is a strictly increasing convex function. Many electric utilities prefer to represent their generator cost functions as piecewise linear equations (i.e., single or multiple segment linear cost functions [23]). The latter form for cost functions is considered here, which is represented by the following equation:

$$\mathscr{C}_j(\hat{P}_j^G) = \alpha + \beta \hat{P}_j^G \tag{4.37}$$

Here α and β represent the cost-coefficients for that particular generator.

In OPF, the objective is to minimize the total generation cost based on expected or estimated loads at different buses. With the loss of generality, this objective is modeled as a constraint which specifies that the cost must be less than a limit, T_{OPF}. This constraint is sufficient to understand the minimum impact of a stealthy attack. The constraint is formalized as follows:

$$\sum_{1 \leq j \leq b} \mathscr{C}_j(\hat{P}_j^G) \leq T_{OPF} \tag{4.38}$$

Notation *OPF* represents the conjunction of the OPF constraints described above.

4.3.3 Formalization of Attack Impact on OPF

4.3.3.1 Change in Loads Due to Stealthy Attacks

According to Eq. (4.9), $\Delta P_j^B \neq 0$ specifies that there is a load and/or generation power change at the bus. This impact model assumes that a change in the measurement of a bus power consumption specifies a change exclusively in the load, which leads to $\Delta P_j^G = 0$. The reason behind this assumption is as follows: The measurement of the power produced by a generator (i.e., the power injected to the bus by a generator) is well-defined, which is changed only if AGC suggests that. Typically, after the estimation of states, if any load change is found, the optimal power flow process (along with contingency analysis) is run, the result of which shows whether (and which) change in the generation is required for optimal efficiency. Therefore, according to Eq. (4.9), the change in the power consumption of a bus specifies the change in the load at that bus. The following equation denotes this:

$$\forall_{1 \leq j \leq b} \ \Delta P_j^D = \Delta P_{j,total}^B$$

Let $\hat{P}_j^D$ be the estimated load (according to the result of state estimation) at bus j, which is also the input to the OPF model. Therefore:

$$\forall_{1 \leq j \leq b} \ \hat{P}_j^D = P_j^D + \Delta P_j^D$$

At a particular bus j, there is usually an expected bound for the load. If $\hat{P}_{j,max}^D$ and $\hat{P}_{j,min}^D$ are the maximum and minimum loads at bus j, the following constraint holds:

$$\forall_{1 \leq j \leq b} \ \hat{P}_{j,min}^D \leq \hat{P}_j^D \leq \hat{P}_{j,max}^D \tag{4.39}$$

4.3.3.2 Impact on OPF

In order to define the increase in the generation cost (i.e., the increase of T_{OPF} in the OPF model), let $\mathcal{T}_{OPF}$ be the optimal cost of generation in the normal (i.e., attack-free) situation. Now, if the attacker's objective is to increase the cost by $I\%$ of the optimal cost, then $T_{OPF} = \mathcal{T}_{OPF}I/100$. Therefore, the constraint to impose the desired impact by launching a stealthy attack is formalized as follows:

$$(T_{OPF} = \mathcal{T}_{OPF}I/100) \rightarrow \neg\, (\exists_{\hat{P}_1^G, \hat{P}_2^G, \dots, \hat{P}_b^G} OPF) \qquad (4.40)$$

The above constraint states that there is no possible allocation of generation that can cost less than T_{OPF}. In addition, since the attacker's goal is not to make the OPF solution fail to converge (possible when the line capacity constraints fail), it must be ensured that there are OPF solutions for larger values:

$$(T_{OPF} \gg \mathcal{T}_{OPF}I/100) \rightarrow OPF \qquad (4.41)$$

4.3.4 An Example Case Study

This example demonstrates the impact analysis model. It is also based on the same 14-bus system as shown in Fig. 4.1. The complete input regarding the example is shown in Table 4.4. The line information includes a set of data for each line: line number, end buses (from-bus and to-bus) of the line, a value indicating the line admittance, the line capacity (i.e., the maximum possible power flow through this line), the knowledge status, and the line status properties: (1) whether this line is included in the true topology, (2) whether its existence is fixed in the topology, (3) whether the topology information regarding this line is secured, and (4) whether the attacker has the ability to alter the data. According to the input, all of the 20 lines are included in the true topology, while lines 4, 14, and 17 are not included in the core topology. The topology mapping information regarding lines 4 and 14 is not secured, while the attacker has the capability to change the topology information regarding all of the lines, except 1, 2, and 3. According to the measurement information, all of the potential measurements are taken except measurements 5, 10, 14, 19, 22, 27, 30, 35, 43, and 52. Measurements taken at bus one are secured. The attacker has access to all measurements that are taken.

The information about the buses in terms of load and generation is also shown in Table 4.4. It is assumed that a generation bus only has a single generator connected. The generation cost of power is followed from the simple linear function as shown in Eq. (4.37). The values of coefficient α and β for each generator are given in the input. Note that these coefficients are taken arbitrarily and do not correspond to the real costs. The total load of the system is 2.0 per unit, i.e., 200 MW (considering a

Table 4.4 Input of the example in Sect. 4.3.4

Topology (line) information
(line no, from bus, to bus, admittance, line capacity, knowledge?, in true topology?,
in core topology?, secured?, can alter?)
1 1 2 16.90 0.30 1 1 1 1 0
2 1 5 4.48 0.30 1 1 1 1 0
3 2 3 5.05 0.20 1 1 1 1 0
4 2 4 5.67 0.30 1 1 0 0 1
5 2 5 5.75 0.30 1 1 1 1 1
. . . .

Measurement information
(measurement no, measurement taken?, secured?, can attacker alter?)
1 1 1 0
2 1 1 0
3 1 0 1
4 1 0 1
5 0 0 0
6 1 0 1
7 1 0 1
. . . .

Attacker's resource limitation (measurements, buses)
28 7

Generator information (bus no, max generation, min generation, cost coefficient)
5
1 1.80 0.20 15 200
2 1.20 0.10 20 220
3 1.60 0.10 25 120
6 1.60 0.20 20 200
8 1.60 0.20 15 140

Load information (bus no, existing load, max load, min load)
11
2 0.20 0.30 0.10
3 0.40 0.40 0.10
4 0.15 0.40 0.05
5 0.15 0.40 0.05
6 0.25 0.40 0.05
9 0.15 0.30 0.05
10 0.10 0.30 0.05
11 0.20 0.30 0.10
12 0.15 0.30 0.05
13 0.15 0.40 0.00
14 0.10 0.30 0.05

Cost constraint, minimum cost increase by attack (in percentage)
412 5

100 MVA base). The cost constraint in the attack-free condition is \$4120 (i.e., there is a satisfied OPF solution in this cost).

In this example, the attacker's objective is to launch a stealthy topology attack, such that he or she can create at least a 5 % increase in the generation cost. In this example, the attacker's resource constraints limit alteration to a maximum of 28 measurements at a time. These measurements can be distributed at no more than seven buses. The execution of the model corresponding to this example returns *sat* along with the assignments to different variables of the model. According to the assignments, the attack vector specifies the following points:

- An exclusion attack on the topology needs to be launched such that lines 4 and 14 are unmapped from the topology.
- States 3, 4, 6, 7, 8, 9, 10, 11, 12, 13, and 14 must be attacked.
- In order to keep this attack undetected, measurements 3, 4, 6, 7, 11, 13, 18, 23, 24, 26, 31, 33, 38, 39, 42, 44, 46, 50, 51, and 53 need to be altered. These measurements are distributed in buses 2, 3, 4, 6, 10, 11, and 13.

The increased generation cost is almost \$4550, which is approximately 10 % more than the optimal value received in an actual (i.e., without attack) scenario.

4.4 Security Hardening Against Stealthy Attacks

The security verification model presented above allows a grid operator to understand potential threats on state estimation with respect to an expected scale of attack (expressed in terms of different attack attributes) and to take necessary security measures accordingly. However, an automated mechanism is needed to generate a security architecture. Although it has been shown that UFDI attacks can be defended if a strategically chosen set of measurements are secured [2, 10], they only consider a specific attack model, where adversaries have perfect knowledge and unlimited capability. Based on this worst case attack model, the set of measurements to be secured can exceed the grid operator's resource (e.g., budget). Therefore, a security design mechanism is required that can provide security within the resources of the grid operator, while keeping the power system state estimation secure with respect to an attack model (i.e., security requirements). This section presents such a mechanism.

4.4.1 Synthesis Design

The mechanism utilizes the verification model to determine a security architecture, which typically includes a list of measurements that must be secured. With respect to the false data injection, a measurement is assumed to be secured if its data integrity is protected. Since securing a number of measurements distributed in

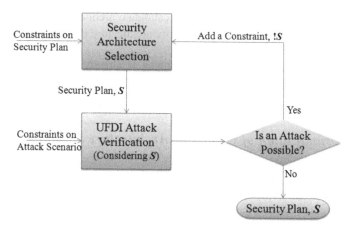

Fig. 4.3 The flow diagram of the security architecture synthesis mechanism for protecting state estimation attack

many substations is very costly compared to a set of measurements distributed in a small number of substations, this mechanism focuses primarily on the substation (i.e., bus) security-based architecture. A secure bus usually means that all of the measurements taken in that bus are secured. A bus can be secured by deploying a PMU (can be multiple for a large bus) at the bus with necessary security measures [4, 5]. Since the PMU can provide the voltage phasor of the bus and current phasors of all the branches incident to the bus, if the PMU is secured then all of these measurements become secured. At the unit level, security is being provisioned by existing PMU vendors [20]. Although the mechanism presented here finds the security architecture as a set of buses to be secured, a similar mechanism can synthesize a security architecture with respect to measurements only.

Figure 4.3 shows the flow diagram of the security architecture synthesis mechanism for resisting state estimation attacks. It is an iterative approach with the combination of two formal models. One of these models is the candidate security architecture selection model. It selects the set of buses as a candidate of the security architecture considering some invariant and user-driven constraints on the security architecture.

The second model is the stealthy attack verification model presented before, which is utilized to verify whether the selected candidate architecture can protect state estimation from UFDI attacks with respect to the security requirements (i.e., an expected attack model). Security requirements are ensured when the verification model returns *unsat* (i.e., no attack vector can be found). If a candidate architecture fails to ensure the required security, a constraint is added to the candidate security architecture selection model so that this architecture is removed from the potential candidate set. The updated model is solved for another candidate architecture and the verification model is used to ensure the security requirements. This process continues until a security architecture is found (i.e., as long as the verification model returns *unsat*). However, when the candidate architecture selection model fails to return a candidate set, then no security architecture is possible according to the given security requirements.

While the stealthy attack verification model is already discussed before, the candidate security architecture selection model is presented below.

4.4.2   Formalization of Candidate Architecture Selection

The main constraint for selecting the buses in the architecture is the resource limitations of the grid operator. The number of selected buses cannot exceed a limit (T_H). If h_j denotes whether bus j is secured, then:

$$\sum_{1 \leq j \leq b} h_j \leq T_H \tag{4.42}$$

Securing a bus implies that all of the measurements that are recorded at this bus are secured. This relation is formalized as follows, when L_j denotes the lines connected to bus j:

$$\forall_{1 \leq j \leq b} \; h_j \rightarrow (t_{2l+j} \rightarrow s_{2l+j})$$

$$\forall_{1 \leq j \leq b} \; h_j \rightarrow \bigwedge_{i \in L_j} (t_i \rightarrow s_i) \wedge (t_{l+i} \rightarrow s_{l+i}) \tag{4.43}$$

The grid operator may have the limitation that he or she is not capable of securing a particular set of buses. Those buses should be excluded from the candidate set, as shown in the following arbitrary example:

$$\neg h_2 \wedge \neg h_6 \wedge \cdots \tag{4.44}$$

Different analytical constraints can be used to limit the search space in the security architecture selection model. As Eq. (4.11) specifies, if the line power flow cannot be changed, the phase difference between the two buses connected by the line cannot be changed. Hence, if a bus is secured (i.e., all the measurements at the bus are secured), the state of a connected bus cannot be changed with respect to the state of the secured bus. Stealthy attacks on the states of these two buses are possible through a third bus which is not connected to the secured one but rather to the other. Therefore, securing the connected bus is not required to protect state estimation of the grid. Equation (4.45) formalizes this constraint.

$$\forall_{1 \leq j \leq b} \; h_j \rightarrow \bigwedge_{i \in L_j} ((f_i = j) \wedge t_i) \rightarrow \neg h_{e_i}) \wedge$$

$$((e_i = j) \wedge t_{l+i}) \rightarrow \neg h_{f_i}) \tag{4.45}$$

Algorithm 1: Security architecture synthesis

1: F_{Attack} formalizes the stealthy attack verification model.
2: F_{Secure} formalizes the security architecture selection model.
3: **loop**
4:     Save (*Push*) current F_{Attack} into $\bar{F}_{Attack}$.
5:     **if** Solver returns a model M (i.e., *sat*) for F_{Secure} **then**
6:         Get the security architecture S from M.
7:     **else**
8:         Exit program.
9:     **end if**
10:    Add security constraints to F_{Attack} based on S.
11:    **if** Solver returns *unsat* for F_{Attack} **then**
12:        Return S.
13:    **else**
14:        Add the constraint $!S$ to F_{Secure}.
15:    **end if**
16:    Retrieve (*Pop*) the saved formalization $\bar{F}_{Attack}$ into F_{Attack}.
17: **end loop**

4.4.3   An Example Case Study

The candidate security architecture selection model is encoded into SMT logics*SMT logic*. Then, the synthesis mechanism is implemented according to Algorithm 1 that utilizes the verification model and the candidate selection model. The algorithm is an iterative process, which stops when a security architecture is found (line 12) or there is no more candidate set available for verification (line 8). The following case study illustrates the security architecture synthesis mechanism. The case study is again based on the IEEE 14-bus test system and three different attack scenarios.

Scenario 1:   The attack model of the first scenario is similar to the first part of the example (attacker's objective 1) as shown in Sect. 4.2.6. In this scenario, the attacker has limited information (i.e., admittances of lines 3 and 17 are unknown). The grid operator can consider such a constraint on the attacker's knowledge, if he or she is certain that the admittance information regarding this set of lines is neither disclosed nor predictable. The attacker also has limited resources, such that he or she cannot attack more than 12 measurements simultaneously. The grid operator, due to resource constraints, can secure four buses maximally. Bus one is considered as the reference bus. In this scenario, the security architecture produced by the synthesis mechanism suggests that buses 1, 6, 7, and 10 must be secured, as shown in Fig. 4.4a (i.e., all the measurements in these buses are data integrity protected). However, there can be different sets of buses, which also can secure the system. The presented mechanism can synthesize all of these sets.

Scenario 2:   In the second scenario, the attacker knows the complete information (i.e., all line admittances) for launching UFDI attacks and he or she has the ability to inject false data into any number of measurements. In this case, there

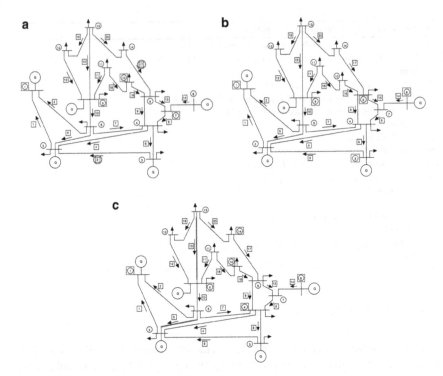

Fig. 4.4 The security architectures (the *green squared* buses needs to be secured) in different scenarios: (**a**) incomplete information (the *red circled* line's admittance is unknown), (**b**) complete knowledge, and (**c**) incorporating with topology poisoning attack (the *red lines* are potential to inclusion or exclusion topology attacks). In all scenarios, bus one is the reference bus

is no solution with four buses that can secure state estimation of the grid against UFDI attacks. If the grid operator can secure five buses, there is a solution. In this solution, the buses to be secured are 1, 3, 6, 8, and 9 (as shown in Fig. 4.4b).

Scenario 3:   This scenario is the worst case situation compared to the last two scenarios. Here, the attacker has complete knowledge of the grid and he or she has the ability to inject false data into any number of measurements. In addition, the attacker can change the topology by injecting false data to the topology information. In this scenario, only lines 5 and 13 are considered vulnerable to line exclusion or inclusion attacks. However, in this case, no solution is possible by securing five buses only. If it is possible to secure 6 buses, then there is a satisfiable security architecture (i.e., buses 1, 4, 6, 8, 10, and 14), which is shown in Fig. 4.4c.

4.5   Proactive Defense Against Persistent Attacks

The idea of MTD has been studied for a decade, especially in the field of cyber security [9]. Typical information technology systems operate in a static environment. Configuration parameters, such as IP addresses, DNS names, network topology, routing entries, security policies, software stacks, etc. remain mostly static over relatively long periods of time. When a system is static, attackers get enough time to know the configuration and behavior of the system, understand the vulnerabilities and corresponding attack vectors, and consequently launch attacks on the system. The same is true for cyber-physical systems like power grids, where the physical and cyber systems are highly static, the operations are fixed, and the protocols are known.

Moving target defense is the concept of controlled change across multiple system dimensions in order to (1) increase uncertainty and apparent complexity for attackers, (2) reduce their opportunity space, and (3) increase the costs of their probing and attack efforts [15]. Usually, MTD is not meant to provide perfect security. The aim of MTD is to enable the operations to be executed safely in a compromised environment, where the system is defensible rather than perfectly secure, particularly against persistent attacks. The attack attributes with respect to stealthy attack are discussed in the beginning of this chapter. The potential of moving target defense mechanisms lies in being able to randomize or perturb one or more of these attributes, where possible. This section presents a moving target defense mechanism considering the knowledge attribute, where uncertainty is added to the information by changing the set of measurements and the topology properties (i.e., line admittances) that consider for state estimation. Due to the uncertainty introduced by the MTD strategy, the attack space significantly reduces, although a persistent attacker may still be successful in launching UFDI attacks.

4.5.1   Moving Target Defense Strategy

In order to increase the uncertainty of the attacker's knowledge about the power grid system with respect to state estimation, the MTD mechanism takes two properties of the system: (1) the set of measurements that are considered in state estimation, and (2) the admittances of a group of lines in the topology.

4.5.1.1   Randomization of the Set of Measurements

In regular practice, a fixed number of measurements is used in the state estimation process. According to the bad data detection algorithms, some of the measurements can be ignored in the process, if they are noisy enough (i.e., bad) relative to the rest of the measurements. An adversary needs to know the set of measurements used in state estimation and alter a group of measurements from the set in order to launch a specific UFDI attack. If the attacker does not know the measurement set correctly, he or she may be unable to identify this group of required measurements perfectly (i.e., one or more measurements can be missing in the group or included without necessity). Therefore, if it is possible to randomize the measurement set used in state estimation by including a number of measurements from the unused (but possible) measurements, the attacker's knowledge about the measurement set becomes uncertain.

For example, the IEEE 14-bus test system [16] has 14 buses and 20 lines. Hence, with respect to the DC power model, it is possible to have 54 measurements (considering forward and backward power flows through transmission lines and power consumption at buses). Among these possible measurements, assume that a fixed set of 30 measurements is taken (i.e., recorded and reported using sensors/meters) for state estimation, while the remaining 24 potential measurements are not. According to the MTD mechanism, a set of 7 measurements, for example, can be taken from the unused measurements by deploying sensors corresponding to those measurements. Then, from the total of 37 measurements, an arbitrary set of 30 measurements can be selected to be used in state estimation. However, the selected set must be capable of observing the system. The later part of this section presents a formal model to select a measurement set according to the observability requirement.

4.5.1.2 Perturbation of Line Admittances

There are distributed flexible AC transmission system (D-FACTS) devices, which can be deployed on transmission lines and are capable of performing active impedance (i.e., reactance) injections [7]. Leveraging this capability of D-FACTS devices, the randomization of line admittances is considered in this MTD mechanism. It is assumed that the admittance of a line can only be randomized if a D-FACTS device is deployed there. However, there are some limitations of using D-FACTS devices. Changes in impedance have impacts on the power flows, which can easily affect the power system operations (e.g., the optimal power flow of the system [14]).

In order to obtain the effect on the power flows due to the deliberate changes in impedance of power lines with the help of D-FACTS devices, a sensitivity analysis related to D-FACTS devices is thoroughly explained in [18]. In the MTD mechanism, the feasibility constraint in changing line admittances must be considered, in which it is ensured that the secured optimal power flow solution remains the same in spite of the changes in the admittances, although some of the power flows must change [14]. It is also required to ensure that the changes cannot be trivial. Further, all the lines with D-FACTS devices will not always be randomized. A set of lines among them will be chosen during each state estimation, and only admittances of these chosen lines will be perturbed. The adversary may know the actual admittance (i.e., base admittance) of each of these lines, although he or she does not know the change amount. Therefore, the changed admittance is assumed to be unknown to the adversary. It is also assumed that when a set of line admittances is changed, the previously changed admittances are returned back to the base admittances. As a result, at a particular time, admittances of only the selected set of lines are unknown to the adversary.

Arguably, power system operations personnel may not be willing to perturb line impedances for the exclusive purpose of detecting attacks. However, D-FACTS-based perturbation of line parameters has been considered for minimization of power system losses and voltage control applications [18]. In practice, such line parameter changes could be leveraged to detect attacks. In the following, the MTD mechanism is illustrated through perturbation of line parameters as exclusively done for attack detection, while keeping in mind that perturbation done for other optimization applications could be leveraged instead.

4.5.2   Formal Model for Strategy Selection

Figure 4.5 shows the architecture of the MTD mechanism. It is a combination of two modules, as shown in the figure: one for the selection of an arbitrary set of measurements for state estimation, and another for the selection of an arbitrary set of lines and corresponding admittance perturbations. This section presents the formal designs of these two modules.

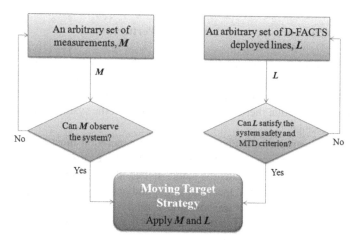

Fig. 4.5 The moving target defense (MTD) mechanism for hardening the security of state estimation

4.5.2.1 Selection of a Measurement Set

The power system is observable when the measurements, each of which represents a power equation, must solve the unknown states. Therefore, Eqs. (4.7) and (4.8) need to be considered as constraints. Now, if a measurement is taken, its power flow or consumption measurement value is assumed to be zero. That is:

$$\forall_{1 \le i \le l} \ (t_i \lor t_{l+i}) \rightarrow (P_i^L = 0)$$

$$\forall_{1 \le j \le b} \ t_{2l+j} \rightarrow (P_j^B = 0)$$

Whether a set of taken measurements can observe the system can be verified as follows. If each of the measurements is considered as zero, all of the states must be the same. This is because the difference between the states of each connecting pair of buses should be zero to make each of these measurements zero. On the other hand, if the system is not observable with this set, then there exists at least a pair of buses which have different states with respect to each other (i.e., nonzero difference). This idea of contradiction is used to prove the observability of a set. The following constraint ensures that all of the states cannot be the same:

$$\exists_{1 \le j_1, j_2 \le b, j_1 \ne j_2} \ \theta_{j_1} \ne \theta_{j_2}$$

Now, if there is no satisfiable solution to this model, it is concluded that the set of measurements can observe the system.

4.5.2.2 Selection of Lines and Admittance Perturbations

In the selection of the lines and corresponding changes in admittances, the main constraint is that the changes need to be done such that the OPF cost does not increase. Specifically, the aim is to keep the generation dispatch as it is according to the existing OPF, so that there is a minimum impact on the system operation due to the topology change.

The main constraint for OPF is that the total generation must be equal to the total expected load. Since the demands at different buses remain unchanged, the required total generation remains the same. Hence, the existing OPF solution can remain optimal after the admittance changes, if and only if the changed power flows still remain within associated transmission limits. Since all the power flow and consumption equations (i.e., Eqs. (4.7) and (4.8)) must hold, they are considered as constraints:

$$\forall_{1 \le i \le l} \ P_i^L = \hat{d}_i(\theta_{f_i} - \theta_{e_i})$$

$$\forall_{1 \le j \le b} \ P_j^B = \sum_{i \in \mathbb{L}_{j,in}} P_i^L - \sum_{i \in \mathbb{L}_{j,out}} P_i^L$$

Here, $\hat{d}_i$ is the changed admittance of line i, such that $\hat{d}_i = d_i + \Delta d_i$, where Δd_i is the change made on line i. The admittance of a line can be changed only if necessary D-FACTS devices are deployed. Therefore, a line is chosen for changing its admittance only if the D-FACTS facility is available there. If h_i denotes whether the line is chosen for admittance change, the following constraint holds on Δd_i:

$$\forall_{1 \leq i \leq l} \ \neg h_i \rightarrow (\Delta d_i = 0)$$

If there is a change in the line admittance, the change cannot be so small that it does not have an impact. If R is the ratio of the minimum change over the line admittance, then the following equation expresses this constraint:

$$\forall_{1 \leq i \leq l} \ h_i \rightarrow (\Delta d_i \geq R \times d_i) \vee (\Delta d_i \leq -R \times d_i)$$

Each line has a capacity for the power flow (i.e., the maximum power that can flow through that line). Let $P^L_{i,max}$ be the line capacity. Therefore:

$$\forall_{1 \leq i \leq l} \ P^L_i \leq P^L_{i,max}$$

The change of a line's admittance is useful to hinder adversaries from launching an attack, if one or more measurements associated with this line are taken. It is worth mentioning that there are four measurements associated with a line: two (forward and backward) line flow measurements and two bus consumption measurements at the end buses. Usually, it is beneficial to take a larger number of measurements associated with a line so that it can have greater impact if the admittance of the line is perturbed. However, this model considers the minimum case as a constraint such that at least one of the measurements associated with the line needs to be taken:

$$\forall_{1 \leq i \leq l} \ h_i \rightarrow m_i \vee m_{l+i} \vee m_{f_i} \vee m_{e_i}$$

The solution to this model verifies whether a given choice of admittance changes on a selected set of lines satisfies the constraints. This model can even synthesize all (or a number of) potential sets of lines for admittance randomization with changed admittance values.

4.5.2.3 Impact of MTD on Attack Attributes

In order to launch a UFDI attack, power flows through various lines and power consumptions at different buses are impacted (i.e., changed by ΔP^L_i and ΔP^B_j amounts, as shown in Sect. 4.2.2). The attacker needs to inject necessary false data to the measurements (i.e., meter readings associated with those power flows and consumptions). However, the attacker only needs to inject necessary false data to measurement i when it is taken. That is:

$$\forall_{1 \le i \le l} (\Delta P_i^L \ne 0) \to (t_i \to a_i) \wedge (t_{l+i} \to a_{l+i})$$

$$\forall_{1 \le j \le b} (\Delta P_j^B \ne 0) \to (t_{2l+j} \to a_{2l+j})$$

The randomization of the set of measurements makes the value of t_i uncertain for the adversary. In addition, if the admittance of a line is unknown to the attacker, he or she cannot determine the necessary changes that need to be applied on the power flow measurements of the line. This condition is formalized as follows:

$$\forall_{1 \le i \le l} (\Delta P_i^L \ne 0) \to ((t_i \vee t_{l+i}) \to g_i)$$

Moreover, when the admittance of a line is perturbed, the admittance is not known to the adversary any more, although the original admittance of the line can be known to the adversary. Therefore, this model considers the following constraint:

$$\forall_{1 \le i \le l} h_i \to \neg g_i$$

4.5.3   An Example Case Study

This section presents a case study demonstrating the performance of the MTD mechanism with respect to stealthy attacks on the IEEE 14-bus test system [16]. *Attackability* is considered as the performance metric in this evaluation. This metric specifies the number of states that can be attacked (i.e., infected by UFDI attacks) over the total number of states.

4.5.3.1   Implementation

The implementation of the MTD mechanism has two major parts: the observability verification model and the line selection model, other than the UFDI attack verification model. Both of these models are encoded into SMT logics, which follow the similar approach like that of the attack verification model which is already discussed before. The solution to the later model generates a number of measurement sets to be used in state estimation. The MTD mechanism randomly chooses one measurement set among them following the uniform distribution. About the line admittance randomization, at first the uniform distribution is used to randomly select a subset of lines among those where the D-FACTS devices are deployed. Then, by executing the line selection model, it is determined whether the admittances of these lines can be changed while satisfying all the necessary constraints.

4.5.3.2   Case Analysis Results

The performance of the MTD mechanism can be shown by analyzing attackability under different scenarios considering access capabilities, knowledge limitations, and security measures. In this case study, two kinds of adversaries are considered: (1) naive and (2) sophisticated. The first type of adversary, as the name indicates, is unaware of the MTD scheme. He or she believes that a fixed set of measurements is used in state estimation. The second type of adversary knows that the MTD mechanism is running at the grid operator's side. As a result, in order to maximize the chances of a successful attack, he or she picks an attack vector that can cover as many potential sets of measurements as possible within resource and access limits. This study considers the same resource constraints for both kinds of adversaries. An adversary can attack 13–15 measurements at a time, while these measurements cannot be distributed over more than 7–8 buses of the system. These results are taken by executing each experiment at least 30 times and taking the arithmetic average of their execution times.

Figure 4.6a shows the attackability (i.e., the number of states that can be attacked out of the total) in three different cases with respect to the application of the MTD mechanism and the adversary type. In the first case no MTD strategy is applied, while in the latter two cases the MTD is used but the type of adversary is different. In the second case the adversary is naive, while in the third case he or she is sophisticated. In these experiments, only the MTD strategy of randomizing the set of measurements used for state estimation is applied. This evaluation is done according to the 14-bus test system, arbitrary 100 sets of 30 measurements from 37 taken measurements, and the accessibility of the adversary varying from 50 to 100 %. It is observed that the attack success probability is always high when there is no MTD. In both of the cases of naive and sophisticated adversaries, the attackability reduces significantly. In the case of a sophisticated adversary, the

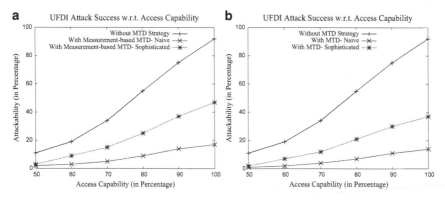

Fig. 4.6 The probability of attack success in the cases of different access capabilities: (**a**) measurement-based MTD strategy and (**b**) measurement and line admittance-based MTD strategy

attackability reduction is smaller compared to that of a naive adversary. This is because the sophisticated adversary uses all available resources to cover as many potential sets of measurements as possible, while the naive adversary only knows one particular set of measurements to be used in the state estimation process. The graphs in Fig. 4.6a also show the impact of the adversary's access capability on attackability. The results are obvious: the lower the attacker's access capability, the better the performance of MTD strategy. In this case, the MTD mechanism is able to reduce attackability down to 5 % when the access capability is no more than 60 %.

Figure 4.6b shows the attackability under different attack capabilities of the adversary, as well. However, in this set of experiments, the MTD strategy of perturbing line admittances is applied along with the randomization of the set of measurements used for state estimation. It is assumed that D-FACTS devices are deployed on an arbitrary set of five lines, while only two lines are chosen among them for admittance perturbation at each time. According to the graphs in Fig. 4.6b, the MTD mechanism shows improved performance when both of the MTD strategies are utilized. This performance improvement is more than 10 % with respect to the measurement set randomization-based MTD alone.

The impact of the adversary's knowledge limitation is analyzed based on the performance of the MTD, with respect to the same three cases: without MTD, MTD with naive adversary, and MTD with sophisticated adversary. Figure 4.7a shows the impact of knowledge limitation when only measurement-based MTD strategy is applied. When the adversary has limited knowledge, MTD strategies perform better. However, the impact of knowledge limitation is significant in the case of the sophisticated adversary. Since a sophisticated adversary leverages knowledge about the system and the MTD strategy in order to increase attack success, when the knowledge is limited to less than 80 %, the success drops significantly.

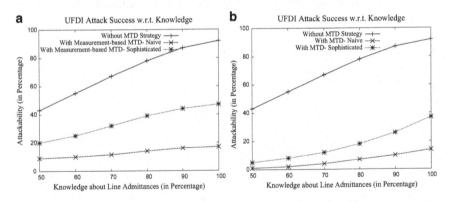

Fig. 4.7 The attackability in the cases of different levels of knowledge about line admittances: (**a**) measurement-based MTD strategy and (**b**) measurement and line admittance-based MTD strategy.

In the case of the MTD mechanism with both randomization of the measurement set and perturbation of line admittances, similar evaluation results (see Fig. 4.7b). However, the significance of the attacker's knowledge limitation is higher in this case. That is, the performance of the MTD increases with the decrease of the adversary's knowledge and this increase is more significant than that of the measurement-based MTD strategy.

4.6 Evaluation

This section presents evaluation results showing the scalability of the formal verification model, as well as that of the security architecture synthesis mechanism.

4.6.1 Methodology

The formal models presented in this chapter are evaluated to analyze their scalability. Simulated experiments are conducted under different problem sizes and the time and memory complexities are observed accordingly. The size of a problem depends mainly on the number of buses, and it is varied by considering different IEEE test systems: 14-bus, 30-bus, 57-bus, 118-bus, and 300-bus [16]. The results presented below are based on experiments that are executed on an Intel Core i5 Processor with 8 GB memory.

4.6.2 Time Complexity of Verification Model

4.6.2.1 Impact of the Problem Size

Figure 4.8a shows the execution time of the UFDI attack verification model with respect to the problem size. The problem size is varied by considering different IEEE bus test systems. Three experiments are performed taking different states to be attacked for each test case. The execution time of each case is shown in Fig. 4.8a using a bar chart. A graph is also drawn using the average execution time for each bus system. It is observed that the increase in the execution time lies between linear and quadratic orders. For a specific bus size, the execution time differs with a different choice of states to be attacked. It is worth mentioning that, although the general problem seems to have a quadratic growth considering the number of buses and the connectivity between them, a smaller execution time is observed. This is because the complexity depends not only on the number of buses, but also on the number of lines, measurements, and attack attributes. An important feature of power grid networks is that the average degree of a node (or bus) is roughly 3, regardless of

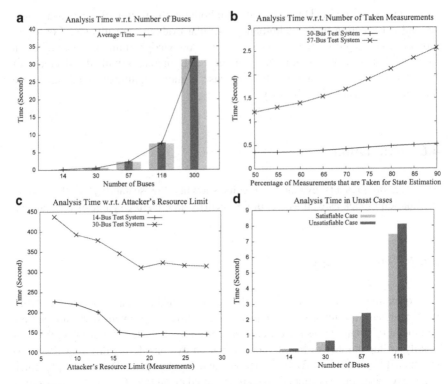

Fig. 4.8 The verification model execution time in different experiments: (**a**) the execution time with respect to the number of buses, (**b**) the execution time with respect to the number of recorded measurements, (**c**) the execution time with respect to the attacker's resource limit, and (**d**) the execution time in unsatisfiable cases with respect to the number of buses

the number of buses in the system [3]. This feature can explain why the complexity is not strictly quadratic.

The impact of the number of taken measurements (represented as the percentage of the total potential measurements) on the model execution time. Figure 4.8b presents the evaluation results for the 30 and 57-bus test systems. The results show that the execution time increases linearly with the increase in the number of taken measurements. Similar results are observed for the other test systems. When the number of recorded measurements increases, the number of measurements to be considered for false data injection also increases, which results in a longer verification time.

4.6.2.2   Impact of the Constraints

The verification of potential UFDI attacks depends on the given constraints, especially the attacker's access capability and resource limit. The impact of the attacker's resource limit on the analysis time is evaluated on IEEE 14- and 30-bus systems. The analysis result is shown in Fig. 4.8c and it is observed that the analysis time decreases with the increase in the attacker's resources (i.e., the resource constraint is relaxed) because the potential of UFDI attacks increases with the increase of the attacker's resources. However, this increase does not help in UFDI attacks after some point (e.g., when the attacker's resource limitation is almost 20 measurements, as shown in Fig. 4.8c). This is because the attacker already has resources which are sufficiently large to launch a UFDI attack to one or more states.

4.6.2.3 Performance in Unsatisfiable Cases

When constraints are tight (e.g., when the attacker can attack a very limited number of measurements), there can be no satisfiable solution. In such cases, the SMT solver often takes a longer amount of time to give the unsatisfiable (*unsat*) results compared to the execution time in satisfiable cases. In unsatisfiable cases, the SMT solver needs to explore the entire solution space to conclude that there is no solution based on the given constraints. Figure 4.8d shows a comparison between the execution times for satisfiable and unsatisfiable cases, with respect to different bus systems. Since different constraints and specific attack goals (corresponding to the attack attributes) are considered for an attacker, the potentiality of an attack vector is already limited. Therefore, the time difference between satisfiable and unsatisfiable cases remains low.

4.6.3 Time Complexity of Impact Analysis

As real values are considered for the attack vector generation, there is usually an extremely large number of stealthy attack vectors possible in an attack scenario. It is seen that finding the impact on OPF, considering such a large number of attack vectors, becomes exceedingly time consuming when the number of buses becomes large. In order to keep the computation cost tractable, the following idea can enhance the efficiency of the formal framework:

Although there can be a larger number of attack vectors, many vectors are close to each other and the difference between them is insignificant with respect to changes in loads. Therefore, it is enough to consider one of these similar attack vectors to see the impact for each of them. According to this idea, the number of attack vectors considered for finding the impact becomes limited, which leads to a reduced execution time. In these experiments, the precision of 2 digits is considered to assume two attack vectors as the same one.

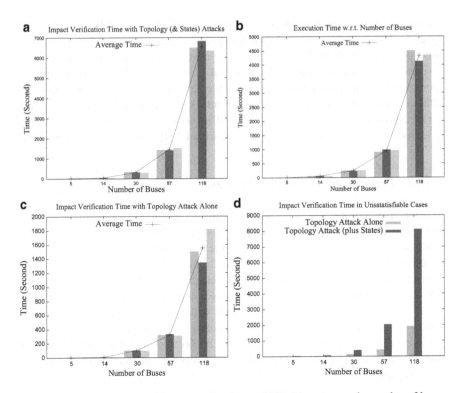

Fig. 4.9 The execution time of Impact verification on OPF with respect to the number of buses in (**a**) UFDI attacks including topology attacks, (**b**) UFDI attacks without topology attacks, (**c**) topology attacks without infecting states, and (**d**) unsatisfiable cases

4.6.3.1 Impact of the Problem Size

Figure 4.9a–c show the execution time for the impact analysis model in different scenarios, considering different kinds of stealthy attacks. The graphs show the impact of the problem size on the execution time. The problem size is varied by considering different IEEE bus test systems. At each problem size, three experiments are performed taking different random scenarios, especially in terms of t attacker's resource limitation. As the attack goal, it is considered to have 2 % increase in the generation cost. The execution time of each of these experiments is shown using a bar chart. A graph is also drawn using the average execution time for each bus system. It is observed that, with respect to the bus size, the increase of the execution time follows exponential order. The execution time of an SMT model depends on the number of variables and the complexity of the theories applied in the model. The number of variables increases with the problem size, particularly in this model due to the number of generators and lines. However, the execution time is much higher in the scenario when infection to the topology and states (Fig. 4.9a) is considered together than the cases when either one of them performed (Fig. 4.9b, c). This is because it is possible to launch multiple attacks on one or more states with respect to a single line inclusion or exclusion attack, which increases the attack space (i.e., search space), significantly. It is worth mentioning that, due to this larger attack space, the second scenario can make larger (and various) impact on OPF compared to the first.

4.6.3.2 Performance in Unsatisfiable Cases

Figure 4.9d shows the execution time in the unsatisfiable cases. With respect to Fig. 4.9a and c, it is obvious that the execution time in unsatisfiable cases is higher than the time in the satisfiable cases. This is because the SMT solver requires verification of all the potential attack vectors in order to conclude that there is no attack that can create the desired impact.

4.6.4 Time Complexity of Synthesis Mechanism

4.6.4.1 Impact of the Problem Size

The execution time of the security architecture synthesis mechanism with respect to different test bus systems is shown in Fig. 4.10a. Two scenarios are considered in the experiments: (1) 90 % of the measurements are recorded for state estimation, and (2) all of the measurements are recorded for state estimation. The figure exhibits that the increase in the execution time is quadratic in order. However, this execution time is significantly longer than that of the UFDI attack verification model (see Fig. 4.8a). This is because, in order to synthesize the security architecture, the verification model may need to be executed many times till a security architecture is found.

Figure 4.10b presents the impact of the number of taken measurements, specified as the percentage of the total potential measurements, on the time of security architecture synthesis corresponding to the 30 and 57-bus test systems. It is observed that, with the increase in the number of taken measurements, the execution time increases linearly. Since the selection of security architecture is based on the buses, any increase in taken measurements does not increase the selection time. However, since the verification time increases with the increase in taken measurements (as shown in Fig. 4.8b), the time for the security architecture synthesis increases.

4.6.4.2 Impact of the Constraints

A security architecture depends on the given constraints (e.g., the attacker's resource limit). The impact of this resource limit, represented as the percentage of the total measurements, on the security architecture synthesis time is shown in Fig. 4.10c. The synthesis time decreases slowly with the increase in the attacker's

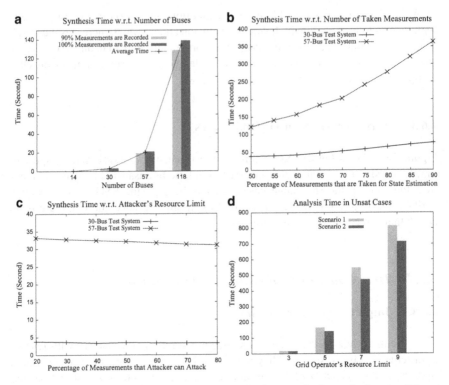

Fig. 4.10 The execution time of the security architecture synthesis mechanism in different experiments: (**a**) the execution time with respect to the number of buses, (**b**) the execution time with respect to the number of taken measurements, (**c**) the execution time with respect to the attacker's resource limit, and (**d**) the execution time in unsatisfiable cases with respect to the number of buses

resource limit value. This is because the increase of the attacker's resources decreases the time to find that a candidate security architecture is unsuccessful, which is actually the satisfiability of the UFDI attack model. As a result, the synthesis time decreases.

4.6.4.3 Performance in Unsatisfied Cases

When the grid operator's resources can be so limited that there is no security solution. The execution time in such an unsatisfiable case is usually high because the synthesis mechanism requires verification of all the potential security architectures to conclude that there is no security solution based on the given constraints. Figure 4.10d shows the execution times of the synthesis mechanism in unsatisfiable cases. This analysis is done based on the IEEE 30-bus test system and by varying the resource limit values in two different scenarios. In the first scenario a security plan needs a minimum number of ten buses, while in the second the number is 12. No

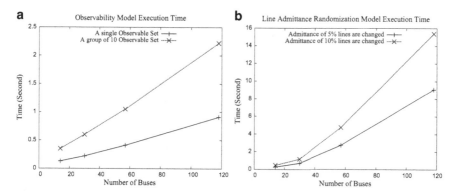

Fig. 4.11 These two graphs shows the model execution time with respect to the number of buses: (**a**) the execution time of the observability model and (**b**) the execution time of the line admittance randomization model

security plan is possible with less than this many buses. The figure shows that the closer the resource limit is to the minimum number of necessary buses, the higher the execution time is to discover that there is no solution. When the limit is too close to the minimum requirement, the unsatisfiability comes at the very end of the search, and thereby the early rejection of a potential search mostly does not take place.

4.6.5 Time Complexity of MTD Strategy Selection Models

The efficiency of the formal models developed for the MTD strategy selection is the results show them as time-efficient. Figure 4.11a shows the execution time of the observability verification model with respect to the problem size, which exhibits that the execution time lies within a few seconds in the case of 100 buses. The execution time of the line admittance perturbation model is presented in Fig. 4.11b, which shows that the model takes approximately 15 s for 100 buses.

4.6.6 Memory Complexity

The memory required by the SMT solver [24] for executing the verification model (refer to Sect. 4.2) and candidate security architecture selection model (refer to Sect. 4.4) is evaluated in different IEEE bus test systems. The memory requirement for an execution of the SMT model depends mainly on the number of variables defined in the model and the number of intermediate variables generated by the solver to implement the satisfiability modulo theories used in the model.

Table 4.5 The required memory space (in MB)

# of buses	Verification model	Candidate selection model
14	1.32	0.05
30	2.60	0.10
57	4.56	0.16
118	9.69	0.31

The memory analysis results are presented in Table 4.5, which shows that memory usage of the formal models increases almost linearly with the number of buses.

The memory or space required by the SMT solver [24] for executing the MTD strategy selection models on the 14-bus test system is presented in Table 4.5. The memory requirement for an execution of the SMT model depends mainly on the number of variables defined in the model and the number of intermediate variables generated by the solver to implement the SMT logics (background theories) used in the model. The analysis results show that the observability model takes less than 4 MB of memory, while the line admittance randomization model needs less than 22 MB of memory.

4.7 Summary

Securing state estimation against cyber-attacks is of paramount importance to maintain the integrity of the power grid. This chapter presents an SMT-based formal framework to systematically investigate potential security threats, particularly the feasibility of stealthy cyber-attacks, on state estimation. An extension of this framework is also presented to find the impact of stealthy attacks on the economic operation of a power system with respect to the OPF module. Thus, this formal framework is capable of modeling stealthy attacks considering an adversary's constraints, analyzing the attack's feasibility, and quantifying consequences in terms of increases in overall generation costs. The framework also allows an operator to capture interdependency among attack attributes to synthesize a security architecture, which secures a set of buses for immunity against UFDI attacks. It is possible to develop an agility-based security solution that introduces uncertainty in the system following the MTD idea. This mechanism applies randomization on the power grid system properties, particularly the set of measurements that is used in state estimation and the admittances of a set of lines. This MTD mechanism includes two formal models to find the observable sets of measurements and the lines for randomizing admittances. The scalability of these models is discussed with case-studies and experiments on different IEEE bus test systems. According to the evaluation results it is seen that these formal models are time-efficient, although with different levels of efficiency. This chapter presents a bunch of formal models which provide a basis for the development of cyber-security tools for modern power grids.

References

1. A. Abur, A.G. Exposito, *Power System State Estimation: Theory and Implementation* (CRC Press, New York, 2004)
2. R. Bobba et al., Detecting false data injection attacks on dc state estimation, in *IEEE Workshop on Secure Control Systems, CPS Week*, Stockholm, Apr 2010
3. D.J. Brueni, L.S. Heath, The PMU placement problem. SIAM J. Discrete Math. **19**(3), 744–761 (2005)
4. J. Chen, A. Abur, Placement of PMUs to enable bad data detection in state estimation. IEEE Trans. Power Syst. **21**, 1608–1615 (2006)
5. J. De La Ree et al., Synchronized phasor measurement applications in power systems. IEEE Trans. Smart Grid **1**, 20–27 (2010)
6. L. de Moura, N. Bjørner, Satisfiability modulo theories: an appetizer, in *Brazilian Symposium on Formal Methods* (2009)
7. D. Divan, H. Johal, Distributed FACTS - a new concept for realizing grid power flow control, in *IEEE 36th Power Electronics Specialists Conference, 2005 (PESC '05)* (2005), pp. 8–14. doi:10.1109/PESC.2005.1581595
8. A. Ipakchi, F. Albuyeh, Grid of the future. IEEE Power Energy Mag. **7**(2), 52–62 (2009)
9. S. Jajodia et al., (ed.) *Moving Target Defense- Creating Asymmetric Uncertainty for Cyber Threats*. Advances in Information Security, vol. 54 (Springer, New York, 2011)
10. T.T. Kim, H.V. Poor, Strategic protection against data injection attacks on power grids. IEEE Trans. Smart Grid **2**(2), 326–333 (2011)
11. D. Kundur et al., Towards a framework for cyber attack impact analysis of the electric smart grid, in *IEEE International Conference on Smart Grid Communications* (2010), pp. 244–249
12. Y. Liu, P. Ning, M.K. Reiter, False data injection attacks against state estimation in electric power grids, in *ACM Conference on Computer and Communications Security (CCS)*, Chicago, IL, Nov 2009, pp. 21–32
13. P. McDaniel, S. McLaughlin, Security and privacy challenges in the smart grid. IEEE Secur. Priv. **7**(3), 75–77 (2009)
14. A. Monticelli, *State Estimation in Electric Power Systems: A Generalized Approach* (Kluwer Academic Publishers, Norwell, 1999)
15. Moving Target Defense (MTD) Cyber Security (2015), R and D Center, U.S. Homeland Security, https://www.dhs.gov/science-and-technology/csd-mtd. Accessed 2015
16. Power Systems Test Case Archive (2015), http://www.ee.washington.edu/research/pstca/. Accessed 2015
17. M.A. Rahman, H. Mohsenian-Rad, False data injection attacks with incomplete information against smart power grids, in *IEEE Conference on Global Communications (GLOBECOM)* (2012)
18. K.M. Rogers, T.J. Overbye, Some applications of Distributed Flexible AC Transmission System (D-FACTS) devices in power systems, in *40th North American Power Symposium (NAPS'08)* (2008), pp. 1–8
19. K.C. Sou, H. Sandberg, K.H. Johansson, Electric power network security analysis via minimum cut relaxation, in *50th IEEE Conference on Decision and Control and European Control Conference (CDC-ECC)* (2011), pp. 4054–4059
20. J. Stewart et al., Synchrophasor security practices (2011), https://www.selinc.com/WorkArea/DownloadAsset.aspx?id=8502
21. A. Teixeira et al., Cyber security analysis of state estimators in electric power systems, in *IEEE Conference on Decision and Control* (2010), pp. 5991–5998
22. O. Vukovic et al., Network-layer protection schemes against stealth attacks on state estimators in power systems, in *IEEE International Conference on Smart Grid Communications* (2011)
23. A.J. Wood, B.F. Wollenberg, *Power Generation, Operation, and Control*, 2nd edn. (Wiley, New York, 1996)
24. The Z3 Theorem Prover, Microsoft Research (2015), https://github.com/Z3Prover/z3/wiki. Accessed 2015

Chapter 5
Intrusion Detection Systems for AMI

Recent studies have shown that AMI is potential to immense number of threats [7, 14, 19, 24, 25], which can affect the deployment and growth of smart grids. These studies outline that although there are some secure communication protocols used in smart grids, many vulnerabilities and exploitations have been observed. Despite these facts, limited progress has been made so far in order to detect malicious behaviors in smart grids [3, 4, 10]. In Chap. 1, Fig. 1.3 presents a typical AMI network. Smart meters communicate with intelligent data collectors using various mediums. These collectors communicate with the headend system (and vice versa) using WAN. Unlike traditional networks, AMI has its own requirements which pose significant challenges for monitoring and intrusion detection. First, sensor deployment in the meters is practically infeasible due to the limited computational power and space resources at the node [23]. Second, although some researchers have suggested the meter-based sensors [3, 10, 27], smart grid providers as well as vendors firmly avoid this option due to the prohibitive cost increase associated with the large number of meter deployments. Therefore, most IDS proposals for the AMI lack practical feasibility.

Deploying detection module at the collector provides the benefit of monitoring both the meter-collector and collector-headend communication. Moreover, AMI communication activity is by default logged at the collector thus it does not pose any extra burden. Although device configuration and log's integrity is protected using headend-collector key-pairing, this AMI feature was never exploited for monitoring and characterizing the AMI behavior. AMI is a special purpose network and its traffic dynamics are often very low since it supports a limited number of protocols and it is configuration-driven. Moreover, there are a limited types of devices in smart grids and a small number of vendors are also involved with these devices. By exploiting this limited variation, simple specification-based intrusion detection techniques are presented in the recent literature [3].

This chapter presents a novel stochastic model checking-based intrusion detection technique. It is designed to fit the requirements and log characteristics of

© Springer International Publishing Switzerland 2016
E. Al-Shaer, M.A. Rahman, *Security and Resiliency Analytics for Smart Grids*,
Advances in Information Security 67, DOI 10.1007/978-3-319-32871-3_5

the AMI. As the AMI behavior is deterministic and can be predicted easily, it allows attackers to evade an IDS by mimicing the behavior. To make it robust against such evasion, a mechanism is presented here that mutate the behavior using the pre-shared secret key which keeps the behavior deterministic for the collector. The AMI infrastructure behavior is modeled using the event logs collected at the collector. This work considers a stochastic model based on fourth order Markov chain for representing the AMI probabilistic behavior because this order exhibits a low conditional entropy. Probabilistic behavior is observed as a result of its configuration and nature of the network. Specifications written in LTL are automatically generated from the a-priori known configurations of the AMI devices (meters and collectors), which in turn are then probabilistically verified using the stochastic model generated from the collector's logs. The presented technique exhibits high accuracy and it can be easily deployed in the existing AMI of a smart grid. An extensive evaluations on a real-world dataset of more than two thousand meters shows promising results for this model, including an accuracy rate of more than 95 % with negligible false alarms of 0.1 %.

5.1   Background

AMI is a core component of a smart grid responsible for the two-way communication between the smart meters and the headend system. A typical network topology of an AMI is shown in Fig. 1.3. HAN is realized as the customer home network which is connected with a smart meter that acts as an interface for a HAN to connect with AMI network. The homes in a neighborhood area create a network area network (NAN), which is responsible for the communication between the intelligent data collectors and the meters. NAN scales from hundreds to thousands of nodes including the meters and the collectors. Lastly, WAN is responsible for the backhaul connectivity between the NAN, i.e., the collectors, and the headend system. As discussed in Chap. 1, different communication channels are often used in AMI. Collectors and meters in a NAN can use wi-fi or power-line communication to interact with each other, while high range and bandwidth technologies are used in WAN for connecting a NAN with the headend system.

Intrusion detection has gained tremendous attention and many anomaly-based IDS techniques have been proposed for cyber systems [11, 12, 15]. However, intrusion detection techniques for AMI needs to be computationally inexpensive because meters do not have enough computation power [23]. If the detection modules are to be deployed as a stand alone unit next to the meter, it requires significantly higher cost. It can be argued that due to this higher deployment cost, industrial deployments of the intrusion detector for the AMI have not been witnessed yet. The solution presented in this chapter is cost effective and practical since it can be deployed either in the headend system or in the AMI.

5.2 Dataset

In AMI, the real-world dataset is important since all of the contemporary work uses simulation which may not necessarily reflect the true behavior of the system under consideration. Therefore, it is very important to analyze a real-world dataset in order to reveal its true behavior. The results presented in this chapter are based on a real-world dataset collected at an AMI of a leading smart grid based utility provider. The experiments are conducted on a smart grid testbed in a controlled environment [8]. The testbed includes a monitoring/management node which is capable of monitoring and configuring the nodes in an AMI, also referred as network management system (NMS). It also includes the multiple meters and collectors, both of which are capable of bi-directional communication.

As it is not practically feasible to capture network traffic in AMI, the event logs generated at the collector are collected as the source of information. Since event logging is an inherent capability of a collector, it does not impose any extra burden on the collector. These logs are saved at collector for sometime and then deleted in a cyclic manner. An offline analysis of the logs is performed in order to avoid any service disruption. Logs of multiple collectors are collected in two sessions, each spanning 1 week. Data collected at these two sessions are denoted as Log-1 and Log-2. Approximately more than 2000 m were communicating with the collectors. The AMI infrastructure used devices from multiple vendors. Sample meter configurations after anonymization are shown in Table 5.1. In this AMI configuration, the reporting mode for the meters is 'push', i.e., a meter sends scheduled readings by itself at the interval specified in the reporting schedule. Energy usage sampling tells the number of seconds after which a sample is taken. Similarly, Table 5.2 shows the configuration of the collectors. It can be observed that the collector is aware of its neighboring meters and the link through which they are connected. In this case study, meters were communicating with the collectors using both the power-line and wireless media. However, the analysis and technique discussed in this work is generic and should hold across other communication models as well.

Sample log entries of a collector are shown in Table 5.3. These entries are simplified and anonymized to show only the information required in this work. Each log entry has the timestamp. The figure shows the relative timestamp with respect to the start of the logging event. However, it is absolute in practice.

Table 5.1 Sample meter configuration after anonymization

Meter	Vendor	Memory (MB)	Usage sample schedule (s)	Reporting time (min)
meter1	vendor1	512 MB	20	1
meter2	vendor1	512 MB	40	1
meter3	vendor2	784 MB	15	2
meter4	vendor3	784 MB	30	1

Table 5.2 Sample collector configuration after anonymization

Collector	Vendor	Neighboring meters	Link type	Reporting time (min)	Buffer size (GB)
SC1	vendor1	meter1, meter2	Link1	1	4
SC2	vendor1	meter3	Link2	2	4
SC3	vendor1	meter4, meter5	Link3	2	6
SC4	vendor2	meter6	Link4	1	6

Table 5.3 Sample log observed at collector

Time (relative)	Source	Destination	Size (KB)	Type (communication)	Relay
388.3709	meter1	SC1	28	0	meter2
602.6901	SC1	meter1	2	0	meter2
633.5265	meter2	SC1	5	3	meter1
388.3709	SC1	meter2	38	2	meter1
732.5435	SC1	meter3	1	1	meter2

Timestamp is followed by the source and destination ID of the nodes involved in the communication event. Size of the communication is also logged in kilo bytes (KB). The type of event is also logged followed by the relaying meter. For the type, 0 represents that it was a meter reading report. $1, 2$ and 3 represents disconnect/reconnect, upgrade and load management communication, respectively. The next section shows the statistical analysis of the logs that forms the basis of the presented model.

5.3 Statistical Analysis and Motivation

This section presents the analysis of a number of statistical properties of the log entries. One relevant property that provided us with interesting insights was the analysis of their temporal dependence. It can be intuitively argued that, as long as the log entries are produced by benign events, the log entries observed should exhibit a certain level of temporal dependence. In case of malicious behavior, perturbations in this dependence structure are flagged as anomalous. Therefore, the level of temporal dependence can serve as an important metric for modeling the log entries.

Autocorrelation measures the on-average temporal dependence between the random variables in a stochastic process at different points in time. For a given time lag (simply, lag) k, the autocorrelation function of a stochastic process X_n (where n is the time index) is defined as:

$$\rho[k] = \frac{E\{X_0 X_k\} - E\{X_0\}E\{X_k\}}{\sigma_{X_0} \sigma_{X_k}} \tag{5.1}$$

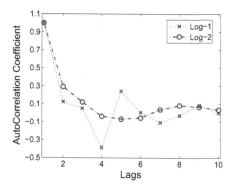

Fig. 5.1 Autocorrelation coefficient trend

Here, $E\{.\}$ represents the expectation operation, σ_{X_k} is the standard deviation of the random variable at time lag k and the stochastic process X realizes the log entries, thus X_n is the log entry at index n. The value of the autocorrelation function lies in the range $[-1, 1]$, where $\rho[k] = 1$ means perfect correlation at lag k (which is obviously true for $k = 0$) and $\rho[k] = 0$ means no correlation at lag k.

Figure 5.1 shows the autocorrelation function plotted against the log entries represented by lags. For both the logs, a certain level of temporal dependence can be easily observed at small lags. This correlation decays in time and eventually drops down to a negligible value. Temporal dependence is present for two reasons. First, meters respond to the collector requests in a short period of time. Second, regular requests and reports are seen thus justifying the homogeneity.

Since log entries are correlated at small lags, they can be modeled using Markov chains. Moreover, it is well-known that a decaying temporal dependence structure can be accurately modeled using Markov chains [20]. Therefore, the concern here is to identify the order of Markov chain model that should be used to accurately model the log entries. To determine the Markovian order, an analysis is conducted on different Markov chain orders. The order can be identified by noting the probabilities at different Markov chain orders. If the probability is low at a given order, the next log entry can be predicted with high accuracy. First, it needs to investigate the probability distribution of log entries at different Markov chain orders and then to use the conditional entropy based measure proposed in [20].

To identify the order of correlation presence in the log entries random process, a Markov chain based stochastic model is needed as follows: Let the log entry tuple at discrete time instance n represents the realization of a random variable derived from a stochastic process X_n. This process is a Markov chain if it satisfies the Markov property, which is defined as:

$$\Pr\{X_n = j \mid X_{n-1} = i, X_{n-2} = i_{n-2}, \ldots, X_0 = i_0\} \tag{5.2}$$

$$= \Pr\{X_n = j \mid X_{n-1} = i\} = p_{j|i}$$

In other words, the probability of choosing a next state is only dependent on the current state of the Markov chain.

In the present context, a Markov chain model X_n is defined for an entry by treating each unique log entry tuple individually and assigning them to non-overlapping bins. Here each unique tuple is assigned to each bin. Therefore, the number of bins will be dependent on the number of unique log entry tuples. Each bin then represents a state of the Markov chain, while the set of all bin indices ψ is its state space. Based on this state representation, a first order Markov chain, $X_n^{(1)}$, can be defined in which each bin represents a state of the random process. Probability of each state i can be calculated by counting the number of times state i occurred and dividing it by the total occurrences of all the states in the Markov chain model X_n. Similarly, an first order Markov chain, $X_n^{(l)}$, can be defined in which each state is an l-tuple $\langle i_0, i_1, \ldots, i_{l-1} \rangle$ representing the values taken by the random process in the last l time instances, i.e., l log entries in this case. In this case the occurrences of l-tuple together will be counted. This will increase the size of state space ψ since different combinations of l-tuple are possible.

Figure 5.2 shows the state probabilities calculated for log entries considering different Markov chain orders, from first to fourth orders. It is clearly observed that as the order of Markov chain increases, i.e., first order to fourth order, total number of states ψ increases, which is the x-axis in Fig. 5.2a–d. However, it gives

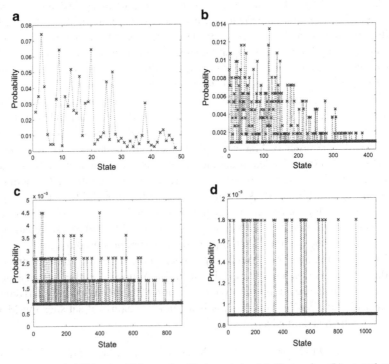

Fig. 5.2 State probabilities for higher order Markov chain. (**a**) First order, (**b**) second order, (**c**) third order, (**d**) fourth order

us an interesting insight that as the order increases, very few states have higher probability of occurrence and rest of the states' probabilities drop to a negligible value. Therefore, using a higher order Markov chain, it is possible to identify the most likely states which will be observed in the logs. Thus it increases the predictability and likeliness of those states. Here, selection of appropriate Markov chain order is important since a higher order yields higher number of possible states and requires more memory. To explore it further, the conditional entropy based measure [20] is used for the log entries for different Markov chain orders. This measure specifies what order of Markov chain can have the most of the information about the next time instance, i.e., log entry.

Conditional entropy, $H(B|A)$, of two discrete random variables A and B charac-terizes the information remaining in B when A is already known. Phrased differently, conditional entropy is 'information about B *not* given by A'. If A and B are highly correlated, most of the information about B is communicated through A and $H(B|A)$ is small. On the other hand, if p_A and p_B (which respectively represent the probability mass functions of A and B) are quite different then $H(B|A)$ assumes a high value, which means that most of the information about B is not given by A. In the limiting cases, $H(B|A) = 0$ when $A = B$, while $H(B|A) = H(B)$ when A and B are independent. The transition probability matrix of the first order Markov chain $P^{(1)}$ can be computed by counting the number of times the state i is followed by state j. The resulting $|\psi^{(1)}|$ histograms can be normalized to obtain the state-wise transition probability mass functions as the rows of $P^{(1)}$.

The conditional probability of the first order Markov chain can be found as:

$$H^{(1)} = - \sum_{i \in \psi^{(1)}} \pi_i^{(1)} \sum_{j \in \psi^{(1)}} p_{j|i}^{(1)} \log_2 \left(p_{j|i}^{(1)} \right), \tag{5.3}$$

Here, $\pi_i^{(1)}$ is the average probability of being in state i which is computed by counting the total number of times each state is visited and then normalizing the frequency histogram.

The measure $H^{(1)}$ defines how much average information is remaining in log entry X_n when it is calculated using log entry X_{n-1}. If the entry is not highly correlated with entries before X_{n-1}, $H^{(1)}$ will be relatively large implying that information about X_n *not* provided by X_{n-1} is high. In such a case, higher first order Markov chain, $X_n^{(l)}$, is used in which each state is an l-tuple $\langle i_0, i_1, \ldots, i_{l-1} \rangle$ representing the values taken by the random process in the last l time instances. Aggregating multiple time instances in a single state allows us to satisfy the Markov property, and hence a transition probability matrix $P^{(l)}$ can be computed by counting the number of times $\langle i_0, i_1, \ldots, i_{l-1} \rangle$ is followed by state $\langle i_1, \ldots, i_{l-1}, i_l \rangle$. The conditional entropy of $X_n^{(l)}$ defined on $\psi^{(l)}$ can then be computed using the same method as (5.3). It is easy to observe that $H^{(1)} \geq H^{(2)} \geq \ldots \geq H^{(l)}$, as each older entry can either be independent of, or provide some information about the present entry. The number of previous entries required to accurately predict the next entry can then be determined by plotting $H^{(l)}$ as the function of the Markov chain order,

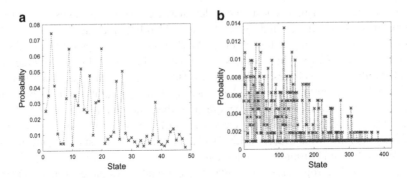

Fig. 5.3 (a) Conditional entropy trend over Markov chain orders and (b) prediction accuracy using fourth order Markov model

$l = 1, 2, \ldots$. The order at which the conditional entropy saturates defines the total number of previous entries which have conveyed as much information of the present entry as possible.

It can be clearly seen in Fig. 5.3a that log entries exhibit a decaying trend over higher order Markov chain. It can be seen that it exhibits an exponential decay trend until the fourth order, which was expected since very few states had higher probability in Fig. 5.2d at the same order. It is clear that most of the information about the next instance is already given at the fourth order since conditional entropy drops to a negligible value, i.e., ≤ 0.2. Therefore, the model uses the fourth order as it gives enough information and increases predictability. The prediction accuracy of the fourth order Markov model is illustrated in Fig. 5.3b. The log data is divided into two halves. The first half is used to learn the model for prediction and the second half is used to test the prediction accuracy. It can be seen in Fig. 5.3b that the model can predict the future log entries with a high accuracy, i.e., $> 95\%$. Therefore, an attacker can easily learn the AMI behavior to devise an evasion technique. In the following section, a robust behavior mutation based technique is presented that minimizes the prediction notion and increases the attack detection.

The results for the third order Markov chain are also shown that exhibit a little lower accuracy but improved scalability since the third order involves with a less number of states. Although the higher order Markov chain exhibits better accuracy but it increases the number of states as compared to the lower order. Therefore, the choice of Markov chain order is a trade-off between scalability (number of states) and accuracy. This is discussed in detail in the later sections, however, the model presented here is built using the fourth order Markov chain.

5.4 Technical Approach

The format of a log entry collected at a collector can be represented as:

$$t, s_{id}, d_{id}, rel, sz, ty$$

Here, t represents the timestamp of the event. s_{id} and d_{id} refers to the source and destination, respectively. However, rel refers to the relaying/forwarding node for the smart meter. It can either be the neighboring meter or meter itself. Let sz and ty denote the size and type of communication, respectively.

The modeling of the AMI behavior for intrusion detection includes the AMI modeling and the property specifications for model checking to verify the presence of intrusions, which are presented below. Finally, a configuration randomization module is presented that counters the evasion and mimicry attacks.

5.4.1 AMI Modeling

The AMI behavior is modeled using collector logs which are generated as a result of randomized configurations. The state of the network is encoded with the following characteristic function derived from the log entry format:

$$\sigma : s_{id} \wedge d_{id} \wedge rel \wedge sz \wedge ty \rightarrow \{true, false\} \tag{5.4}$$

The function σ encodes the state of the network by evaluating to *true* whenever the parameters used as input to the function correspond to the log entry in the collector. If the AMI observes five different log entries, then exactly five different assignments to σ function will result to *true*. Since each collector is independent, the Markov model is learned for each collector separately.

A labeled Markov chain (LMC) is a tuple $M = \{Q, \Sigma, \pi, \tau, L\}$, where Q is a finite set of states, π is an initial probability distribution τ is the transition probability function and L is a labeling function. Atomic propositions AP are assigned to states by a labeling function using $\Sigma = 2^{AP}$. Each state was assigned a unique label derived from σ, which is used to define the state. A probability distribution for sequence of states can then be defined using Markov chain.

Set of states Q is strongly connected if for each state pair (q_i, q_j) there exist a path $q_0, q_1, \ldots, q_n$ such that $q_h \in Q$ for $0 \leq h \leq n$, $\tau(q_h, q_{h+1}) > 0$, $q_0 = q_i$, and $q_n = q_h$. Therefore, if Q is strongly connected, then M is said to be strongly connected. A distribution π_M^s is a stationary distribution for M if it satisfies

$$\pi_{(q)}^s = \sum_{\acute{q} \in Q} \pi^s(\acute{q}) \tau(\acute{q}, q)$$

In order to keep the history of previously visited states, it requires to compute the probability suffix automata (PSA). A PSA is an extended LMC with a labeling function $H : Q \rightarrow \Sigma^{\leq N}$, which represents the history of previously visited, at most N, states. However, if the history is fixed to N, i.e., $\Sigma^{=N}$, the LMC will be called $(N+1)th$ order Markov chain since it includes the current state too. Therefore, each state q_i will be associated with a string s_i such that $s_i = H(q_i)L(q_i)$.

Since the AMI system under consideration is a real-time system and can not be restarted with different initial states, the model learning technique should be able to start observing data from the system at any given time and can work with a single long sequence of observations [6]. The sequence $S = \sigma_1, \sigma_2, \ldots, \sigma_n$, $\sigma_i \in Q$, where σ represents a state as shown in Eq. (5.4). Since the statistical analysis showed that conditional entropy is negligible at fourth order, the model uses the fourth order Markov chain. A finite state machine having directed graph can be learned from the given sequence S. Each state in the graph at time i will be represented by a tuple of 4, i.e., $\langle \sigma_{i-3}, \sigma_{i-2}, \ldots, \sigma_i \rangle$, where σ_i is the $L(q_i)$ and the rest are $H(q_i)$. Therefore, it can be realized as s_i in the finite state machine.

Algorithm 2 explains the learning of a Markov model from the given sequence of log entries. It initializes an empty graph and then starts observing the sequence S. It utilizes a sliding window approach where window slides at instance i by one entry, i.e., σ. However, the size of window to observe $s_i \in S$ is kept to four which is the order of model. If s_i already exists in graph then a directed edge from s_{i-1} to s_i is created, if the directed edge does not exist already. However, if s_i does not exist in graph, then a node is also created for s_i. This process keeps repeating until S is empty. Once the state machine is created, it is easy to calculate the transition probability matrix for that. For each state s_i in graph, $\sum_{\forall \sigma_i \in \Sigma} \tau(s_i, \sigma_i) = 1$.

Since a log entry σ is a conjunction of different variables, total possible combinations can exceed and may require a lot of processing power. However, it

---

Algorithm 2: Learn Markov model

Data: Sequence S
Result: Finite state machine based on fourth order Markov Model
Initialize empty Graph;
$S = \{\sigma_i | \forall \sigma_i \in \Sigma\}$;
$\forall \sigma_i \Pr(\sigma_i) > 0$;
while $S \neq \phi$ **do**
   | Slide window by one σ at instance i ;
   | Pick $s_i \in S$;
   | **if** $s_i \in Graph$ **then**
   | | Make directed edge from s_{i-1} to s_i ;
   | **end**
   | **else**
   | | Create node s_i in Graph ;
   | | Make directed edge from s_{i-1} to s_i ;
   | **end**
end

---

can be calculated for each network under consideration. In this case study, 10 bits were assigned to s_{id} and d_{id}, 4 bits for relay, 8 bits for sz and 3 bits for type ty of communication. Therefore, the possible number of σ are $2^{10} \times 2^{10} \times 2^4 \times 2^8 \times 2^3$ which is a relatively large number. Since the model treats each collector's log separately, either source or destination of each log entry will be fixed to the id of that particular collector. Moreover, a collector can only be connected to its neighboring nodes/meters. In this case study, the collector was connected to 8 other devices. Therefore, the number of σ reduces to $1 \times 8 \times 8 \times 2^8 \times 2^3$, which is relatively smaller. Since fourth order Markov model is being used, possible combinations of four σ can yield to a lot of states. To this end, Algorithm 2 only takes the combinations which are observed in the sequence S and only keeps the edges which are observed since all the combinations are not possible due to configuration, thus reducing the size of transition probability matrix.

5.4.2 Properties Specification for Model Checking

Since the AMI configuration is modeled based on Markov chain and exhibits a temporal dependence, the properties are defined in LTL [2]. Unlike traditional model checking, stochastic model checking allows you to check that with what probability the property is satisfied by the model. These probabilities can be thresholded in order to accommodate the unseen behavior up to a certain extent. LTL over the alphabet Σ is defined by the syntax:

$$\varphi ::= true \mid \sigma \mid \varphi_1 \wedge \varphi_2 \mid \neg\varphi \mid \bigcirc \varphi \mid \varphi_1 \cup \varphi_2 \quad (\sigma \in \Sigma)$$

The derived additional operators $\square$ (always) and $\diamond$ (eventually) are also used in the LTL. Let φ be the LTL formula over Σ. An LTL formula can be satisfied for a sequence of alphabets s which is a state definition in this case having $s = \sigma_1, \sigma_2, \ldots, \sigma_n$ where $\sigma_i \in \Sigma$. Therefore, the probabilistic LTL can be defined as:

$$\phi ::= P_{\bowtie p}(\varphi), \quad \bowtie \ \in \{\geq, >, \leq, <, =\}; \ \ p \in [0, 1]; \ \varphi \in LTL$$

Since the system under consideration is an online system and can not be restarted with a specific initial state, the stationary distributions are applied for satisfiability. LTL properties can be verified with the Markov chain model built in the earlier section. For example, if a configuration parameter defines the sampling rate and report size, a property can be written that whenever a report request is received the reply should have this particular size. Temporally it can be stated that given the system is in 'request' state, the next expected state is 'reply with size h'. In the PRISM model checker tool [22], the 'next' state operator is defined using 'X'. For the given state, one can 'filter' the state space to 'current' state only. Thus, a small parser is developed to read the configuration and to generate the properties in LTL format for the tool.

The properties can be derived from the configurations and the security control guidelines such as NISTIR 7628 [21]. Since the configurations shown are related to reading reports, some examples of the properties derived from the configuration are presented below. Let γ be the number of meters associated with a collector. One basic example is that whenever a report reading request is generated, a meter should respond with a report. It can be formulated as:

$$\phi ::= P_{\geq d_1}(rrep_i|rreq_i), \;\; 1 \leq i \leq \gamma \tag{5.5}$$

where $rreq_i$ and $rrep_i$ represents the reading request and reading report, respectively, for meter i. However, d_1 is used as a probability threshold that this property should be satisfied with the probability greater than or equal to d_1. The property defined here is in conditional probability syntax, however, it can be represented in LTL as:

$$P_{\geq d_1}(\square(rreq_i \rightarrow \bigcirc rrep_i)) \tag{5.6}$$

This is a strict property since it says that the *next* state has to be the $rrep_i$. However, a relaxed property can be defined as:

$$P_{\geq d_1}(\square(rreq_i \rightarrow \lozenge rrep_i)) \tag{5.7}$$

which says that eventually $rrep_i$ will be seen once $rreq_i$ is observed. The strict property (Eq. (5.6)) in the experiments. Similarly, it can also be defined that the report generated should have a size with in the limits defined since sampling rate is fixed. It can be formulated as:

$$\phi ::= P_{\geq d_2}(rsz_i|rrep_i), \;\; 1 \leq i \leq \gamma \tag{5.8}$$

where rsz_i denotes the report size for meter i. However, $rsz_i \in sz_i$ which is a valid report size set for meter i. Moreover, Eqs. (5.5) and (5.8) can be combined to show the temporal behavior, i.e., whenever a reading request is generated, it is followed by the reading reply which has a valid size.

Moreover, a meter should not send the reading report twice in the next T_1 consecutive time periods. It can be formulated as:

$$\phi ::= P_{\leq d_3}(rrep_i|rrep_i), \;\; 1 \leq i \leq \gamma \tag{5.9}$$

where d_3 is thresholded with $\leq$ that the probability of seeing such a behavior should be less than d_3. Suppose t_1 is a counter which observe values in the range $\{1, 2, \ldots, T_1\}$. Equation (5.9) can be represented in LTL as:

$$P_{\leq d_3}(\square \, rrep_i \rightarrow (\neg rrep_i \cup t_1 \geq T_1)) \tag{5.10}$$

To avoid flooding the collector with reports from multiple meters at the same time, the associated meters were configured to have different reporting intervals.

Therefore, collector will not receive consecutive reports from multiple meters in consecutive T_2 time periods. It can be formulated as:

$$\phi ::= P_{\leq d_4}(rrep_j | rrep_i), \; i \neq j, \; 1 \leq (i,j) \leq \gamma \tag{5.11}$$

this prevents the multiple meters from sending the reports after each other for consecutive T_2 time periods. It can be represented in LTL as:

$$P_{\leq d_4}(\Box \, rrep_i \rightarrow \neg rrep_j \cup t_2 \geq T_2), \forall_{j=1}^{\gamma} \tag{5.12}$$

To introduce the unpredictability notion for the attacker, a meter can not select the same neighboring meter for relaying the report in consecutive T_3 time periods. It can be represented as:

$$P_{\leq d_5}(\Box \, rel_{i,j} \rightarrow \neg rel_{i,j} \cup t_3 \geq T_3), \forall_{i,j=1}^{\gamma} \tag{5.13}$$

where $rel_{i,j}$ represents that meter i relayed the report via meter j. Similarly, to avoid conflict and introduce randomness, a meter j can not be selected by multiple neighboring meters, i.e., i and k for relaying the report in a given time window T_4. This also reduces the possibility for a meter to become overwhelmed by its neighboring meters. It can be represented as:

$$P_{\leq d_6}(\Box \, rel_{i,j} \rightarrow \neg rel_{k,j} \cup t_4 \geq T_4), \forall_{k=1}^{\gamma} \tag{5.14}$$

Moreover, the thresholds d_x are learnt from the model built using the benign logs collected under normal condition, i.e., without any attack. However, they can also be manually configured based on the requirements of the network under consideration. Similar to the reading report property specifications, as shown above, other types of configurations are also specified the same way using LTL. These properties are dependent on the configuration of the network under consideration.

5.4.3 Randomization Module

This section discusses the configuration randomization for smart meter configuration. Let γ is the number of neighboring meters associated with a collector c. A range of values, instead of a fixed value, is used for the configuration parameters. Here, three configuration parameters of a meter, i.e., report size, reporting interval, and relaying node are discussed. Sampling rate defines the size of the report. The basic operational constraint is that both the collector and meter should have a unique pre-shared key. The set of constraints on the assigned ranges is discussed below, which is followed by the mutation algorithm.

Random Relay Mutation Meters send the reports to headend through collector. However, to reach the associated collector they may use a neighboring meter as a relay. The mutation can be applied by selecting a random neighbor meter for relaying the report to associated collector. The mutation can defend against reconnaissance and DoS attacks since the meter will use random neighbor to relay the report.

The following constraints should be satisfied for random relay mutation:

- A unique neighbor should be assigned to every meter in every time window (*Unique Assignment Constraint*).
- A same neighbor should not be selected in two consecutive time windows by a meter for relaying (*Non-repeat Constraint*).
- No meter should get more than U_r relaying requests at any given time window (*Capacity Constraint*).

The constraints are formalized for T consecutive time windows. The set $U = \{1, 2, \ldots, \gamma + 1\}$ is defined to be the index of all meters and the collector, where index i ($1 \leq i \leq \gamma$) is the index of meter m_i and $\gamma + 1$ is the index of the collector. The set U_i ($U_i \subseteq U$) is used to denote the set of indices of neighbors of meter m_i.

The *Unique Neighbor Constraint* can be formalized as follows:

$$\sum_{j \in U_i} w_{ij}^t = 1, \ 1 \leq i \leq \gamma, 1 \leq t \leq T \tag{5.15}$$

$$(j \notin U_i) \Rightarrow (w_{ij}^t = 0), \ 1 \leq i \leq \gamma, 1 \leq t \leq T$$

$$0 \leq w_{ij}^t \leq 1, \ 1 \leq i \leq \gamma, 1 \leq t \leq T, 1 \leq j \leq |U_i|$$

In the above equations, w_{ij}^t is the indication variable. If $w_{ij}^t = 1$ then the jth element in U_i will be assigned to meter m_i in time window t, otherwise the jth element in U_i is not assigned to meter m_i in time window t.

The *Non-repeat Constraint* can be formalized as follows:

$$(w_{ij}^t = 1) \Rightarrow (w_{ij}^{t+1} \neq 1), \tag{5.16}$$

$$1 \leq i \leq \gamma, 1 \leq j \leq \gamma + 1, 1 \leq t \leq (T - 1)$$

The *Capacity Constraint* can be formalized as follows:

$$\sum_{i=1}^{\gamma} w_{ij}^t \leq U_r, \ 1 \leq j \leq \gamma, 1 \leq t \leq (T - 1) \tag{5.17}$$

An SMT solver (such as Yices [26]) is used to find the satisfying neighbor assignment for these constraints. In most cases, there are more than one satisfying assignment. The set of satisfying forwarding neighbors of meter m_i in time window t is denoted as U_i^t.

Random Report Size and Interval Mutation Since the mutatation is done randomly on the report size and interval, sz and int are dentoed to be the set containing all the possible valid configuration values for report size and interval respectively, where sz_i^t and int_i^t is the randomly selected configuration value at time t for meter i.

To guarantee the maximum randomization of choices for report sizes and intervals at any time period, the range size (the number of values in a set) for report sizes and intervals should be greater than some threshold. This can be formalized as (*Size Constraint*):

$$|sz_i| \geq \theta \qquad (5.18)$$
$$|int_i| \geq \varepsilon$$

Here, θ and ε are calculated based on the collision probability in the next t time instances, which can be thresholded by the AMI provider.

To guarantee a certain delay between consecutive reports to avoid flooding, all intervals should be greater than a minimum value (*Flooding Constraint*):

$$\forall int_i^t \in int > sz_i/b_i \qquad (5.19)$$

Here, b_i and sz_i are the bandwidth channel and report size for meter i.

To avoid the overflowing of a meter's memory, a report must be pushed less than certain time interval in which memory is not filled by the sampling for report size (*Meter Memory Overfull Constraint*):

$$\forall int_i^t \in int < mem_i/sr_i \qquad (5.20)$$

where mem_i and sr_i are the memory and sampling rate for meter i.

To accurately measure the energy usage, there is a requirement on a minimum sampling rate for meters. This minimum sampling rate differs for different meters, however, a de-facto minimum standard value is 128 samples/s. Since report size depends on the sampling rate, the sampling rate should not fill the buffer in the given reporting interval period. This can be formalized as (*Maximum Sampling Rate Constraint*):

$$\forall sr_i^t < mem_i/int_i \qquad (5.21)$$

To guarantee unpredictability among k consecutive time periods, it is required that the assigned report size and interval should not be the same as that in the previous k time periods. This can be formalized as (*Non-repeat Constraint*):

$$sz_i^t \neq sz_i^{t-j}, \ 1 \leq j \leq k \qquad (5.22)$$
$$int_i^t \neq int_i^{t-j}, \ 1 \leq j \leq k$$

To avoid the DoS attack at the collector, the following aggregate constraints are defined. If all the meters associated with a collector pick the minimum reporting interval and maximum reporting size (worst case), it should be less than the memory and reporting interval of collector to headend.

$$\frac{\sum_{i=1}^{\gamma} sz_i^{max}}{\forall_{i=1}^{\gamma} int_i^{min}} < \frac{mem_{sc}}{int_{sc}} \tag{5.23}$$

where mem_{sc} and int_{sc} are the memory size and reporting interval of collector to headend. However, its a worst case scenario and the constraint can be relaxed in practical:

$$\sum_{i=1}^{\gamma} \frac{\sum sz_i}{l} < mem_{sc} \tag{5.24}$$

It calculates the expected report size for each meter and sum it for all the meters to get the aggregate report size.

5.4.3.1   Mutation Algorithm

To make the behavior deterministic for collector, a pre-established hash function H can be used. In order to make the behavior non-deterministic for the attacker and deterministic for collector, the pre-shared key k_i between meter and collector are taken along with the timestamp t and current values of rate and interval as the input to the hash function.

$$sz(t + 1) = H(k_i, t, sz_i^t) mod\ l\ + 1 \tag{5.25}$$

$$int(t + 1) = H(k_i, t, int_i^t) mod\ j\ + 1 \tag{5.26}$$

$$rel(t + 1) = H(k_i, t, U_i) mod\ |U_i|\ + 1 \tag{5.27}$$

where sz_i^t and int_i^t denotes the current value of report size and interval, respectively, for meter i at time t. The modulus function is used on the result of the hash function to generate a random configuration value within the allowed range. A high level working of the algorithm is shown in Algorithm 3.

5.5   Evaluation

This section discusses the experimentation and evaluation of the configuration randomization technique presented above with respect to an attack model.

Algorithm 3: Mutable configuration

Data: Interval range *int* and report size range *sz*
Pick a size from range *sz* /* `Equation (5.25)`   */
Pick an interval value from *int* /* `Equation 5.26`   */
while *timeCounter* < *int* **do**
    if *sample* < *size* **then**
       | KeepSampling();
    end
end
Select relay neighbor from *U* /* `Equation 5.27`   */
SendReport();
Reset *timeCounter*;
Repeat Process;

5.5.1 Attack Model

Since this technique depends on the logs collected at a collector, attacks which do not involve any communication with the collector or do not create a log entry would not be detected. However, affect of such attacks would be limited to a particular area. In short, this technique is suitable for the large scale attacks which include compromising a large number of meters to cause a major blackout in the area. These attacks can be spoofing, DoS, DDoS, scanning, penetration, evasion, mimicry, etc. A DoS attack, for example, can be launched against the collectors or its associated meters, which can cause the service disruption in the area. Similarly, a DDoS attack on the large number of meters or collectors can cause a major blackout in the wider area.

Since the infrastructure exhibits a deterministic behavior and it is homogenous in nature, spoofing, mimicry, and evasion techniques can inject similar traffic without being detected and thus resulting in the destabilization of the infrastructure. In mimicry attacks, a number of meters can be compromised and operated as they are legitimate. In the recent literature [18], it is shown that meters send the authentication password in the clear text. It is also shown that spoofing and replay attacks are possible. It is intuitive that evasive mimicry attacks, which mimics the behavior, would not be detected by the existing AMI detector [3] since it follows the protocol specification to detect the intrusions. However, mimicry attacks mimic the behavior and will follow the protocol. The basic assumption here is that the key is stored in a trusted platform module (TPM) which can not be accessed by other processes [5]. For example, randomizing the time interval would defend against the replay attacks since the communication will not be expected by the collector at the replay time. Similarly, type and size parameters will defend against the spoofing and the mimicry attacks since the attacker wouldn't know what type and size of communication is expected by the collector at a given time. Moreover, randomizing relay node will defend against the DoS and reconnaissance attacks since attacker would not know that at a given time which relay node to use for the communication. Since multiple parameters are randomized, it will be hard for the attacker to guess/predict all the parameters at a given time in order to stay evasive. Therefore, it makes it harder for the attacker to mimic the normal behavior and stay evasive.

Traditional attacks like denial of service will be detected by the property (5.10) as it will create multiple entries in a time windows shorter than $T1$. Similarly, distributed denial of service will cause the property (5.12) to be invalid since it will cause multiple sources to create log entries in a time window shorter than $T2$. If a penetration attack is launched against the AMI, it will be detected depending on the attack graph. If the penetration is supposed to go through the collector or it tampers with the meter (by changing the configuration), it will be detected since the meter will not behave according to the a priori known configurations. Similarly, malware that tampers with the meter configuration will be detected as well. It is worth mentioning that data injection attacks that only tamper with the usage information will not be detected in this case. However, this work is not focused on the energy theft by individual users. Intrusion detectors specially designed for detecting individual user's energy theft have been proposed recently [17, 18].

To evaluate the randomization technique, attacks are generated in a controlled environment in the smart grid testbed. These attack scenarios include not only different attack types but also different attack locations. Since the home area network has access to the smart meter, two scenarios are considered for this location: (1) compromising the meter and tamper with its configuration, and (2) launching DoS, scanning, evasion, mimicry, and false data injection attacks considering meter as the entry points to AMI. For scanning and DoS, low rate attacks (i.e., 0.1–1 pkts/s) are used. Both the above mentioned scenarios were implemented for these attacks. For evasion, mimicry and spoofing, a switch is placed in between the meters and collector; and attached an attack machine to it. A simple program is written that uses the same configuration as that of a meter and generate similar reading reports in the same format. In order to be evasive, less than 5 % of the total generated traffic by the machine was injected traffic and 95 % was the mimic traffic. For mimicry and spoofing attacks, all the traffic was mimic traffic without any injected traffic. Injected traffic includes malicious commands like random file uploads, requesting reports at irregular intervals (requesting report itself is not an attack), administrative commands without proper authorization and failed authorization attempts. These logs were collected from the collectors and were labeled as malicious. Malicious logs were mixed into the real-world logs collected at an AMI of the utility provider for the purpose of the accuracy evaluation. It was made sure that the volume of malicious logs do not exceed 10 % in the mixed log (benign and malicious).

5.5.2 Robustness Against Evasion and Mimicry Attacks

This section discusses the effectiveness of randomization module against evasion and mimicry attacks. Since evasion and mimicry attacks leverage the known behavior of the network, they tend to stay below the radar to go undetected. Due to the homogenous and deterministic nature of the network, it is not difficult for an attacker to learn the behavior. Therefore, a configuration parameter is randomized such that it becomes difficult for the attacker to guess its value. The reporting interval, size, and relay configuration parameters are randomized. These parameters are mutated every time a report is sent. Since it uses the pre-shared key for randomization, collector does the same computation in order to verify if the parameters values are as expected or not. Behavior compliance of these configurations is checked using the properties defined in the same section.

Robustness of the presented approach against evasion depends on two factors: (1) the probability threshold used in the verification properties, and (2) the configuration parameter randomization. Since a configuration parameter (e.g., reporting interval) is verified by a threshold-based property, a low threshold-based evasion is possible to a certain extent when a significant deviation is allowed. For example, if the property threshold is 0.9, it means that 90 % of the reports should be in the correct time and 10 % can be deviated to accommodate any unexpected network behavior as learnt from the log training. Thus, attackers can leverage this 10 % to launch mimicry and evasion attacks. If the key is not known to attackers, an attacker has to accurately guess the configuration parameters from a range of values such that success ratio will be above the property threshold in order to evade detection. However, this accuracy (evasion) is highly dependent on the parameter randomization range and how many parameters are randomized. For example, if the range defined as 10 min, for reporting interval parameter, in discrete intervals of 1 s each, then the probability that the attacker can guess the correct time interval (attack probability) is as low as 0.0017. Furthermore, the probability of guessing all the parameters, at a given time, would be much less as it is a product of probability of guessing each parameter accurately, which makes it much harder for the attacker to evade by accurately guessing. In order to evade the detection, the attack probability must be greater than or equal to the property threshold. However, this case is extremely unlikely unless randomization range is poorly selected and/or the property threshold has been immaturely determined based on improper training data set.

To analyze the normal behavior of the AMI, the log data received from the utility provider is used. Mutable logs were collected by applying mutable configuration in a smart grid test lab [8]. Multiple smart meters were connected to the collector. NMS was used for configuration management. collector uses a proprietary communication protocol built on top of $C12.22$ protocol. To apply mutable configurations on a meter, script was written in C language using the API of NMS. However, the presented mutation methodology should be embedded in the meters.

The goal of the presented methodology is to increase the randomness of smart meter's behavior using mutation to make the prediction harder for the attacker. Randomness of a distribution can be characterized using entropy, i.e., higher randomness yield to higher entropy value. To evaluate the approach, the conditional entropy is calculated over different Markov chain order for normal logs (utility provider) and mutable logs (testbed).

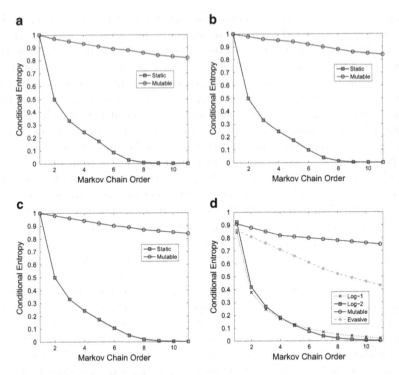

Fig. 5.4 Conditional entropy for static and mutable configuration. (**a**) Relay configuration, (**b**) interval configuration, (**c**) size configuration, (**d**) combined

AMI exhibits a predictable behavior as shown in Fig. 5.3b. The same predictor is applied on the mutable logs (testlab). The prediction accuracy was below 10 % in the mutable configuration environment. Therefore, an attacker can not predict with high accuracy about the next communication instance and its properties like size, interval and relay. The conditional entropy is calculated (Eq. (5.3)) over different Markov chain order for the static and mutable configuration. It can be clearly observed from Fig. 5.4 that mutable configuration has higher conditional entropy than static configuration. Therefore, it can be stated that the mutable configuration introduces sporadic changes in the AMI behavior as opposed to the static configuration, thus making it more random and hard to predict for the attacker. Figure 5.4a–c shows the conditional entropy for relay, report interval and report size respectively. Figure 5.4d shows the conditional entropy for the entire tuple, i.e., conjunction of the three parameters. 'Log-1' and 'Log-2' denotes the real-world logs using static configuration. A steep decaying trend was observed for both the logs which eventually reveals the predictable nature of the behavior given few previous observations. On the other hand, 'Mutable' log did not show a steep decaying trend. Therefore, it is intuitive that mutation is harder to predict to launch an evasive attack.

To launch an evasive mimicry attack against mutated configuration, the predictor is used to generate traffic similar to mutable configurations in a testbed, i.e., it learns and predicts the future states of mutable logs. An attack machine is connected with the switch between the meters and collector. Predicted (mimicry) and actual mutable configuration logs were merged and collected at the collector. Merged (predicted and mutation) activities are labeled as 'Evasive' in Fig. 5.4d. Since prediction accuracy was low, 'Evasive' showed a much steeper curve as compared to the 'Mutable' configuration. This change in behavior ('Mutable' and 'Evasive') helps in differentiating between mutable configuration and prediction for mimicry/evasive attacks. Therefore, it can be concluded that the behavior is hard to learn for an attacker to predict since prediction probability is low.

5.5.3   Accuracy Evaluation

The basic premise of this presented solution is to provide a model using the logs of collector that can verify the configuration properties written in LTL. If a property is verified against the model with probability $p > d$, where d is set as a threshold, it is a normal case, otherwise, it is anomalous. Threshold d was learnt separately for each property by noting the property verification probability using the benign logs model (without attack).

Logs were collected from the collectors which were connected to the multiple meters. Before discussing the accuracy evaluation, a discussion is presented for the basic behavior of the three randomly selected meters for two scenarios, i.e., when the mutable configurations are known and not known to the system. It gives us interesting insight about the temporally deterministic behavior. Then, it is analyzed to find out how well the model represents the system behavior. Please note that this temporal behavioral analysis was done without the attack traffic. The model checking was conducted using a probabilistic symbolic model checker tool PRISM [22].

5.5.3.1   Temporal Behavior of the Model

Since the model preserves the temporal behavior, the properties can be seen as the conditional probability, i.e., $P(A|B)$, where state B has already been observed (given). Therefore, it can be stated as 'what is the probability of seeing state A given state B?'. It can be easily written in the LTL using the 'next' or 'eventually' operator for the state A by filtering all the states except the current/given state, i.e., B as discussed in an earlier section.

Figure 5.5 shows the conditional probabilities given that the request was made for a particular meter for the usage reading and load management as shown in Fig. 5.5a, b, respectively. Although the results are for three meters only, similar results were observed for the other meters as well. Figure 5.5a shows the probability

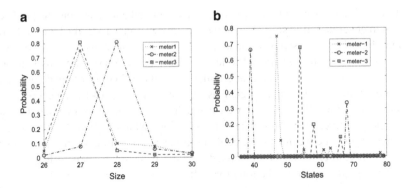

Fig. 5.5 Response probabilities when a request was generated for reading and load management. (a) Response for reading request, (b) response for load management request

of response size, given that the system was currently in the reading request state, i.e., a usage/reading request was sent to a meter. It can be seen that all the three meters generated response within the range of 26–30 KB with different probabilities. Two meters generated response of size 27 KB with higher probability and the third meter generated response of size 28 KB. These responses belong to different states in the model since size was used as a variable in the tuple (σ) used for the state definition. However, none of the meter generated a response of size more than 30 or less than 26 KB which was set as a variance boundary. The reading response size depends on the sampling rate of the meter. Since the response size of the reading request was within the range, the property 'whenever a reading request is generated, the next observed state is reading response with the size modeled' (combining Eqs. (5.6) and (5.8)) was verified with the probability 1. Here the probability 1 can be realized as the sum of all the probabilities of the states having size within the range of 26–30 KB. Please note that the system can be in one state at a given time, i.e., either request sent to meter 1 or meter 2. These conditional probabilities were calculated separately for the next state given that the system was in the request state.

Similarly, Fig. 5.5b shows the next state transition probabilities given that the system was in a load management request state. It can be seen that all the three meters probabilistically responded to the request. Meter 2 (green line with circular marker) showed the two transition probabilities. Response of size 9 KB with probability close to 0.65 and size 6 KB with probability close to 0.35. Similarly, meter-1 responded with six different sizes. All of these sizes were within the range of 5–10 KB. Lastly, meter-3 responded with the three different sizes where one size was most likely and the other two were less likely. It can be observed that whenever the system was in a load management request state, the response state was observed next with the probability of 1. However, response also had multiple states depending on the size of the response which was used as a variable in defining the state s consisting of multiple σ. Therefore, it can be concluded that the model

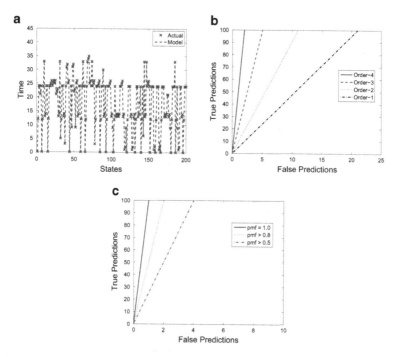

Fig. 5.6 Prediction accuracy for different Markov chain order and pmf for fourth order model.
(**a**) Model prediction, (**b**) different Markov chain order, (**c**) varying pmf on fourth order model

exhibits a temporally deterministic behavior for the system under consideration. It is
clear that the temporal probabilities for the properties can be learnt from the model
built using the benign logs. In the following, it is analyzed whether the model truly
represents the system or in other words how well the model represents the logs.

5.5.3.2 Model Accuracy

In order to determine whether the model actually represents the logs or not, an
experiment is conducted as shown in Fig. 5.6. It does not include the attack traffic or
property verification. The benign logs are divided into two halves. The first half was
used to build a model using Algorithm 2. Second half was used as the test dataset
and the model was applied on it for the prediction. For each step, the current state
was learned and based on the current state, the next state was predicted using the
model, i.e., states having higher probabilities in probability mass function (pmf)
were predicted. Figure 5.6a shows the prediction using the fourth order model. The
red cross marker denotes the actual states observed in the test log. However, blue
dashed line represents the prediction of the model. It can be observed that the model
predicts the future states with high accuracy though few false predictions (less than

1 %) were encountered as well. These false predictions were observed as a result of the unseen behavior since the benign log was divided into two halves. As a result, few lower probability states were not observed after a certain state in the first half and this causes false predictions. To check the model confidence, the prediction was done using 1 h learning to 1 week learning. In all the cases, the false predictions observed were below 1 %.

The results are shown in Fig. 5.6b, c based on different criteria. The total number of predictions were counted and classified whether they were true or not. In Fig. 5.6b, different Markov chain orders are considered where the current state was defined using one tuple or multiple tuple history. It can be observed in Fig. 5.6b that the fourth order Markov chain provides the best prediction accuracy as compared to the lower order Markov chains. Another experiment changed the pmf bound that used for the prediction. For example, pmf of 0.5 means minimum number of next transition states having a probability sum of 0.5. If there are three possible next states based on the current state and they have probabilities 0.6, 0.2, and 0.2, respectively, only the state having probability 0.6 will be selected as the 'predicted' state as it has the probability greater than or equal to 0.5. However, if none of the states has probability higher than 0.5, minimum number of multiple states will be selected whose sum reaches 0.5. Figure 5.6c shows the prediction accuracy for the different pmf. It can be seen that pmf of 1, i.e., based on the current state all the next possible states in the model are predicted, provides the best accuracy with a very low false prediction rate. It can be intuitively argued that this false prediction rate will be the bound for the false positive for the attack detection accuracy, since this shows how well the model represents the data. Therefore, it can be concluded that the fourth order Markov chain can accurately model the underlying network with minimal loss, hence the fourth order is used for the model checking.

5.5.3.3 Detection Accuracy

Mixed data was used to calculate the detection accuracy which had attack and benign logs both. Since the attack logs were generated separately in a controlled environment, the timestamps of the attack logs were adjusted by a fixed constant to have the same time window as of normal or benign logs. Allowed values for the communication type (ty) were used for the attack logs as other communication types do not exist in the model and can be detected easily. For attack detection, model learning was done in a continuous online learning fashion using a sliding window approach. The size of the sliding window was kept to 1 h and the sliding window interval was set to 1 min. Model was learnt separately for each collector in the dataset and detection results were averaged. Figure 5.7a shows the detection accuracy achieved by the presented model. It can be seen that high detection rate of more than 95 % was achieved with a negligible false alarm rate of approximately 0.1 %. Logs were collected from collectors for approximately 2000 m. Average false alarm rate varies from 0.35 to 0.50 false alarms per meter per week, depending upon the threshold used for detection rates > 70 %. It worth mentioning that these rates

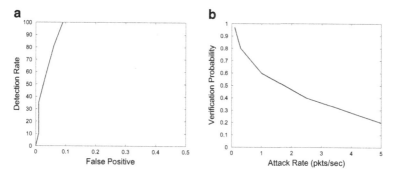

Fig. 5.7 Detection accuracy and verification probability vs attack rate. (**a**) Detection accuracy, (**b**) probability vs attack rate

are on the entire dataset collected. The utility provider from which the log data has been collected has hundreds of thousand smart meters in a state. This might increase to millions of meters in a state for large-scale providers. These could be managed by one or multiple headend systems. Receiver operating characteristics (ROC) curve is generated by changing the verification probability (threshold) of configuration-based LTL properties which were verified against the model built using the mixed data logs. It is intuitive that the attack activity does not follow the state transitions as allowed in the temporal properties. Therefore, the higher volume of attack activity as compared to the benign activity can be easily detected even with the loose probability verification threshold. On the other hand, the lower volume of attack activity will be detected by the strict probability verification threshold. Figure 5.7b shows the effect of verification probability for multiple degrees of DoS attacks. It is observed that a high attack rate is detectable with a loose verification probability threshold.

Complexity of the probabilistic model checker (i.e., PRISM) for a Markov chain model and LTL property verification is doubly exponential in the size of LTL formula and polynomial in the size of state space [16]. Algorithm 2 was implemented in Java on a dual core machine to learn the model from the logs. The run-time complexity is in hundreds of milliseconds ($\approx$ 300 ms) and the memory size of the model for each collector was few kilobytes ($\approx$ 20 KB). The complexity was measured using HPROF [13] tool. Model was then verified against the LTL properties using PRISM. The run-time complexity of the properties verification is approximately 1.5 s.

The presented model can be used in two fashions: (1) use a centralized approach and build a single giant model for the entire AMI, defining collector in either source or destination, the model can reduce the state space to possible states only for that particular collector, in this case offline model checking can be done in the headend by pulling the logs, (2) if the giant state machine exceeds the scalability limit of the model checker, each collector can be modeled separately. In case of modeling each collector separately, the model checking can be done online or offline, depending on the computational power available. Therefore, the presented approach is flexible.

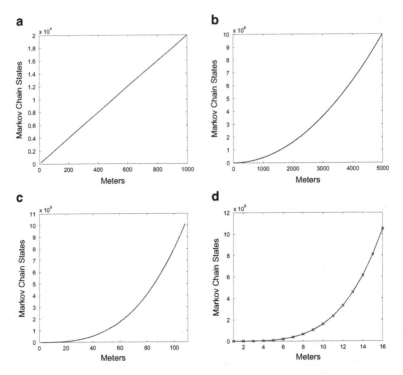

Fig. 5.8 Meters vs number of states. (**a**) First order, (**b**) second order, (**c**) third order, (**d**) fourth order

5.5.4 Scalability

PRISM is shown to be scalable up to 10^{10} states [22]. The maximum number of meters that can be handled with various Markov chain orders are also investigated as shown in Fig. 5.8. The observed results for multiple Markov chain orders, i.e., 1 to 4 are presented in Fig. 5.8. For the first order Markov chain, it can be observed from Fig. 5.8a that the number of states increase linearly with the number of meters. In this case, it can accommodate up to 25,000 m per collector, although up to 1000 m are considered in the graph in order to show the linear trend.

Similarly, the second order Markov chain can handle up to 5000 m as shown in Fig. 5.8b. It is observed that the order tends to be exponential. Scalability for third and fourth order Markov chain is shown in Fig. 5.8c, d, respectively. It can be clearly observed that both the Markovian orders increase the state space exponentially with the increase in number of meters. More specifically, the third and fourth order Markov chains can work up to 108 and 16 m, respectively.

Since many vendors use 8–16 smart meters per collector, it is found that using the fourth order Markov chain is the optimal choice to maximize accuracy. It is also found that many major vendors use similar limited number of meters per collector due to limited bandwidth (in power-line communication) and coverage (in WiFi communication) [1, 9]. However, vendors might support different models of the AMI technologies that offer different capacity of handling meters. For example, some smart grid providers/vendors plan to use other technologies that can support hundreds of meters per collector [9].

For this reason, two approaches are discussed here that offer much more scalable solution but with reasonable accuracy sacrificing. First, third order Markov chain can be used since it also incurs a low conditional entropy as shown in Fig. 5.1b. Moreover, it shows acceptable prediction accuracy, with slightly more false predictions as compared to fourth order as shown in Fig. 5.6b. Second, the fourth order Markov chain approach is extended to handle more meters by state compression. Moreover, logs can also be divided based on the group of meters (16 in each) to conduct the analysis.

It can be seen from Fig. 5.2d that very few (only tens of) states are highly likely (high probability) out of 1000. Thus, eventually less than 10 % states are seen more frequently than others. Therefore, once the graph is made using Algorithm 2, a compression algorithm is run to remove the nodes having lower probability. The detection accuracy is performed using the compressed model and note that it incurs an increase in the false positive rate, i.e., from 0.1 to 0.2 % while maintaining the same detection accuracy. However, the compressed state model can easily scale to more than 1000 m per collector. Choosing the appropriate alternative approach depends on the AMI network technology under consideration.

The computational cost and scalability of the mutation algorithm are also evaluated. The Fig. 5.9a shows the SMT solving time for the constraints with different numbers of meters per collector. U is the number of average neighbors for every single meter. Solving time is almost linear with the number of meters per collector, and the number of neighbors has only negligible effect. The Fig. 5.9b shows the SMT solving time for the combination of unique neighbor assignment, non-repeat and meter capacity constraint with different meter capacity. r is the

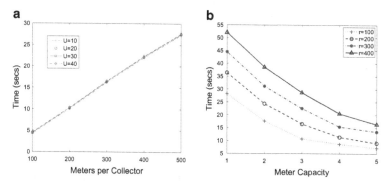

Fig. 5.9 Computational time for SMT formalization for mutation algorithm. (**a**) Randomization computation vs No. of meters, (**b**) randomization computation vs meter capacity

number of meters for every collector. It is seen that the solving time increases when the number of meters per collector increases, and decreases when meter capacity increases. This is because when the meter capacity increases, it is easier for the solver to find satisfiable solutions.

The mutation scheme is shown for the three configuration parameters, however, it can be extended to more. Since the configuration mutation randomly picks a configuration value from a given range, the larger the size of the range, easier it is to satisfy the mutation constraints. It can be seen in Fig. 5.9b that as the meter capacity to handle more relay request increases, the computational cost to satisfy constraint decreases. Therefore, the approach is scalable to hundreds of meters per collector. However, in practice tens of meters per collector are used. This case uses 8 neighboring meters as relay, 80 different sampling rates ranging from 128 to 208 samples/s, 105 different reporting intervals ranging from 15 to 120 s.

5.5.5 Limitations

This section discusses the limitations of the presented approach briefly. The original fourth order Markov chain based approach only scales up to 16 m per collector. In actual, a collector may have higher number of meters associated with it. To combat this, an alternative solution has been presented in Sect. 5.5.4 which supports up-to 1000 m per collector while incurring a slight increase in false alarm rate. Moreover, the original approach can also be used by dividing a collector's log into multiple chunks based on the groups of smart meters. Each chunk may have up to 16 m grouped into it. This can easily be done by filtering the log based on the meter id.

Attacks which do not involve communication with a collector will not be detected. However, the effect of such attacks is expected to limited to a particular area, i.e., not large scale. Evasion robustness relies on the key used for mutation. It can be assumed that the key is secured and attacker can not access it. However, if the key is compromised, attacker can evade the detection algorithm by generating similar traffic using the key if the mutation algorithm and configuration parameters are known. The technique provides robustness against evasion, however, an attacker that has full access to and complete knowledge of the AMI may still be able to evade it.

5.6 Summary

This section presents a fourth order Markov chain based model for intrusion detection since it incurs lower conditional entropy and higher prediction accuracy. Moreover, it fits the state space requirement of the AMI network under consideration. The uniqueness of the model lies in the configuration-based stochastic modeling of the AMI using the logs collected at collector and device configuration.

Moreover, considering the challenges of AMI network, the presented approach is practical since it does not require high computation power and memory in the field. This technique can also work offline in the substation by pulling the collector logs from the area. Therefore, it is flexible and incurs low cost. However, if collectors provide enough computation and memory, it can be deployed in parallel. It also does not need to be trained, unlike traditional intrusion detectors. The model provides acceptable detection accuracy of more than 95 % with false alarm rate close to 0.1 %. The model is extensible according to the AMI network under consideration using more information in the logs and configurations. Therefore, the scope is not limited to what is presented here.

References

1. Ambient Smart Grid Nodes (2013), http://cdn2.hubspot.net/hub/165743/file-20041060-pdf/docs/ambient_smart_grid_node.pdf
2. C. Baier, J.P. Katoen, *Principles of Model Checking* (The MIT Press, Cambridge, 2008)
3. R. Berthier, W. Sanders, Specification-based intrusion detection for advanced metering infrastructures, in *IEEE 17th Pacific Rim International Symposium on Dependable Computing (PRDC)* (2011)
4. R. Berthier, W. Sanders, H. Khurana, Intrusion detection for advanced metering infrastructures: requirements and architectural directions, in *First IEEE International Conference on Smart Grid Communications (Smart-GridComm)* (2010)
5. D.C. Challener et al., Storing keys in a cryptology device, US Patent Application 10/051,495, 2002
6. Y. Chen et al., Learning Markov models for stationary system behaviors, in *NASA Formal Methods*. Lecture Notes in Computer Science (Springer, New York, 2012)
7. F.M. Cleveland, Cyber security issues for Advanced Metering Infrastructure (AMI), in *IEEE Power and Energy Society General Meeting-Conversion and Delivery of Electrical Energy in the 21st Century* (2008)
8. Duke Energy Smart Grid Laboratory (2015), http://epic.uncc.edu/laboratories/duke-energy-smart-grid-laboratory. Accessed 2015
9. Echelon Data Concentrator (2013), http://www.echelon.com/assets/bltdc1832fafd7deb8c/Data-Concentrator-DCN-1000-Series-datasheet.pdf
10. M.A. Faisal et al., Securing advanced metering infrastructure using intrusion detection system with data stream mining, in *Proceedings of Pacific Asia Workshop on Intelligence and Security Informatics (PAISI)* (2012)
11. P. García-Teodoro, J. Díaz-Verdejo, G. Maciá-Fernández, E. Vázquez, Anomaly-based network intrusion detection: techniques, systems and challenges. Comput. Secur. **28**(1–2), 18–28 (2009)
12. Y. Gu, A. McCullum, D. Towsley, Detecting anomalies in network traffic using maximum entropy estimation, in *Proceedings of the ACM SIGCOMM Conference on Internet Measurement (IMC)* (2005)
13. HPROF: A Heap/CPU Profiling Tool (2015), http://docs.oracle.com/javase/7/docs/technotes/samples/hprof.html. Accessed 2015
14. Idaho National Laboratory (INL), NSTB Assessments summary report: common industrial control system cyber security weaknesses, May 2010
15. J. Jung et al., Fast portscan detection using sequential hypothesis testing, in *Proceedings of the IEEE Symposium on Security and Privacy* (2004)

16. M. Kwiatkowska, D. Parker, Advances in probabilistic model checking, in *Proceedings 2011 Marktoberdorf Summer School: Tools for Analysis and Verification of Software Safety and Security* (2012)
17. D. Mashima, A.A. Cárdenas, Evaluating electricity theft detectors in smart grid networks, in *Research in Attacks, Intrusions, and Defenses* (2012)
18. S. McLaughlin, D. Podkuiko, P. McDaniel, Energy theft in the advanced metering infrastructure, in *Critical Information Infrastructures Security* (2010)
19. S. McLaughlin et al., Multi-vendor penetration testing in the advanced metering infrastructure, in *Proceedings of the 26th Annual Computer Security Applications Conference, (ACSAC)* (2010)
20. M. Merhav, M. Gutman, J. Ziv, On the estimation of the order of a Markov chain and universal data compression, in *IEEE Transactions on Information Theory* (1989)
21. NISTIR 7628: Guidelines for Smart Grid Cyber Security, Smart grid inter-operability panel- cyber security working group (2010), http://www.nist.gov/smartgrid/upload/nistir-7628 _total.pdf
22. Probabilistic Symbolic Model Checker, PRISM (2015), http://www.prismmodelchecker.org/. Accessed 2015
23. Smart Meter - ARM (2015), http://www.arm.com/markets/embedded/smart-meter.php. Accessed 2015
24. The White House, Homeland Security Presidential Directive 7: Critical Infrastructure Identification, Prioritization and Protection (2003). Last published on 22 September 2015, while originally published on 17 December 2003. See https://www.dhs.gov/homeland-security-presidential-directive-7
25. U.S. Government Accountability Office (GAO), Information security: TVA needs to address weaknesses in control systems and networks (2008)
26. Yices: An SMT Solver (2015), http://yices.csl.sri.com/. Accessed 2015
27. Y. Zhang et al., Distributed intrusion detection system in a multi-layer network architecture of smart grids. IEEE Trans. Smart Grid 2(4), 796–808 (2011)

Appendix A
Resiliency Threat Analysis for SCADA

This chapter presents a formal model that automatically verify the resiliency of the SCADA system, particularly the resilient data acquisition for reliable execution of control operations. This formal model can verify the system with respect to the given resiliency specifications, as similar to the model presented in Chap. 3. While the previous solution looks for the satisfaction of the resilient observability constraint, this formal model searches for threat vectors that fail the resiliency requirement. The unsatisfiable outcome certifies that the system is resilient with respect to the specified resiliency.

A.1 *k*-Resilient Secured Observability Threat Model

The notations used in the following formal modeling are followed from those defined in Chap. 3. The modeling of the resiliency threat verification needs to utilize the secured data delivery constraint.

Secured Data Delivery The assured data delivery constraint (as defined in Chap. 3) verifies whether data can reach from the source to the destination, e.g., from a field device to the MTU, through zero, one, or more intermediate devices, but does not ensure if the transmission has occurred under necessary security measures. Although this constraint checks security pairing between the communicating parties, it is only to ensure necessary handshaking for communication. The secured data delivery constraint (*SecuredDelivery*) verifies whether data is sent under proper security measures, particularly authentication and integrity protection, including the assured data delivery. That is, the communicating nodes, e.g., an RTU and the MTU, may have correct security pairing, as they are using the same security protocol Challenge-Handshake Authentication Protocol (CHAP). However, this security pairing on CHAP only ensures authentication. In this case, the transmission will not

© Springer International Publishing Switzerland 2016
E. Al-Shaer, M.A. Rahman, *Security and Resiliency Analytics for Smart Grids*,
Advances in Information Security 67, DOI 10.1007/978-3-319-32871-3

be data integrity protected. Moreover, it is required to consider the vulnerabilities of the security measures in use. For example, if Data Encryption Standard (DES) is used for data encryption, the transmitted data cannot be considered as protected, as a good number of vulnerabilities of DES have already been found.

The formalization of the secured data delivery includes two more constraints, *Authenticated* and *IntegrityProtected*, that ensure the authentication of the communicating parties and the integrity of the transmitted data, respectively. The following equation presents the formalization of secured data delivery:

$$\exists_K (\exists_k CryptType_{i,k} = K) \wedge$$
$$(\exists'_k CryptType_{i,k'} = K) \wedge$$
$$((CAlgo_K = hmac \wedge CKey_K \geq 128) \vee \ldots))$$
$$\rightarrow Authenticated_{i,j}$$

$$\exists_K (\exists_k CryptType_{i,k} = K) \wedge$$
$$(\exists'_k CryptType_{i,k'} = K) \wedge$$
$$((CAlgo_K = sha2 \wedge CKey_K \geq 128) \vee \ldots))$$
$$\rightarrow IntegrityProtected_{i,j}$$

$$Ied_l \wedge$$
$$\exists_z \forall_{l \in |\mathscr{P}_{l,j,z}|} \ \{i',j'\} \in NodePair_l \wedge$$
$$Node_{i'} \wedge Node_{j'} \wedge Reachable_{i',j'} \wedge$$
$$CommPropPairing_{i',j'} \wedge CryptoPropPairing_{i',j'}$$
$$Authenticated_{i',j'} \wedge IntegrityProtected_{i',j'}$$
$$\rightarrow SecuredDelivery_l$$

The main difference between this formalization of *SecuredDelivery* and that presented in Chap. 3 is that the sides of the implies relation exchanged. This is because, unlike the previous modeling, this formal modeling is designed to look for the cases that make the secured observability fail.

Failure of Secured Observability The secured measurements are logically identified from the mappings between communicating field devices and measurements. Whether the system is observable securely is verified using the mappings between the secured measurements and the states. Let S_Z be a Boolean variable denoting whether measurement Z is secured. Then, the following two conditions ensure if measurement Z is secured:

$$\forall_{l \in IedSet} \forall_Z \ (Z \in MsrSet_l \wedge SecuredDelivery_l) \rightarrow S_Z$$

If a measurement is secured, the variables corresponding to this measurement can be securely estimated. If SE_X denotes whether state X is securely estimated, then the following must hold:

$$\forall_Z \ \forall_{X \in StateSet_Z} \ S_Z \rightarrow SE_X$$

The set of securely delivered unique measurements (with respect to $UMsrSet_E$) needs to be identified. Let $SecUMsr_E$ be this set. Then, it is formed as follows:

$$\forall_E \ \exists_{Z \in UMsrSet_E} S_Z \rightarrow SecUMsr_E$$

The secured observability (*SecuredObservability*) ensures that the minimum number (i.e., at least m) of secured measurements are received and all states are covered by these secured measurements. Thus, the system is securely unobservable (¬*SecuredObservability*) when either or both of the following two conditions fail:

$$\neg SecuredObservability \rightarrow$$

$$(\exists_X \ \neg SE_X) \vee (\sum_E SecUMsr_E < m)$$

k-Resilient Secured Observability Threat This constraint verifies whether secured observability is ensured even if k field devices (or k_1 IEDs and k_2 RTUs) are unavailable due to technical failures or cyber attacks. The verification of k-resilient secured observability is verified by searching for threat vectors under the specification of maximum k failures. When the number of unavailable devices is no larger than k devices (or k_1 IEDs and k_2 RTUs), the threat against the k-resilient secured observability constraint (¬*ResilientSecuredObservability*) is formalized as follows:

$$((N - \sum_{1 \leq i \leq N} Node_i) \leq k) \wedge \neg SecuredObservability$$

$$\rightarrow \ \neg ResilientSecuredObservability$$

$$((N_1 - \sum_{1 \leq i \leq N} (Node_i \times Ied_i)) \leq k_1) \wedge$$

$$((N_2 - \sum_{1 \leq i \leq N} (Node_i \times Rtu_i)) \leq k_1) \wedge$$

$$\neg SecuredObservability$$

$$\rightarrow \ \neg ResilientSecuredObservability$$

The threat vector (**V**) includes a list of devices such that if they fails the secured observability is impossible. In this way, this proposed modeling synthesizes attack vectors and, thus, provides inputs to learn the dependability breach points.

A.2   A Case Study

This section presents an example that illustrates the execution of the model in two synthetic attack scenarios. These scenarios demonstrate the k_1, k_2-resilient secured observability constraint.

SCADA Topology 1   This example considers the 5-bus SCADA system as shown in Fig. 3.5 of Chap. 3. The input is partially shown in Table A.1. The input includes primarily the Jacobian matrix corresponding to the bus system, the connectivity between the communicating devices, the association of the measurements with the IEDs, and security profiles of each communicating host pair. Each row of

Table A.1 The input to the case study

Number of states and measurements
5 14
Jacobian matrix (mapping between the states and the measurements)
0 -5.05 5.05 0 0
0 -5.67 0 5.67 0
0 -5.75 0 0 5.75
0 0 0 -23.75 23.75
16.9 -16.9 0 0 0
4.48 0 0 0 -4.48
0 5.67 0 -5.67 0
0 5.75 0 0 -5.75
0 0 5.85 -5.85 0
0 0 0 23.75 -23.75
-16.9 33.37 -5.05 -5.67 -5.75
0 -5.05 10.9 -5.85 0
0 -5.67 -5.85 41.85 -23.75
-4.48 -5.75 0 -23.75 37.95
Number of each type of devices in the topology
IEDs (Id 1-8), RTUs (Id 9-12), MTU (Id 13), Router (Id 14)
8 4 1 1
Topology (Links)
13 #Number of communicating links
1 9
2 9

(continued)

Table A.1 (continued)

---

3 9

. . . .

Measurements corresponding to IEDs

1 1 2

2 3 5

3 11

4 12

5 4 7 9

6 13

7 6 8 10

8 14

Security profile (if exists) between the communicating entities

11 # Number entries of security profiles

1 9 hmac 128

2 9 chap 64 sha2 128

3 9 chap 64 sha2 128

5 11 chap 64 sha2 256

6 11 chap 64 sha2 256

7 12 chap 64 sha2 128

8 12 chap 64 sha2 128

9 13 rsa 2048 aes 256

10 11 hmac 128

11 13 rsa 4096 aes 256

12 13 rsa 2048 aes 256

k-resiliency requirements (IED, RTU)

1 1

---

the Jacobian matrix corresponds to a measurement. The first row corresponds to measurement 1, and similarly the rest. Each row has five entries (columns) which correspond to five buses or states. It is assumed that the measurements are recorded by different IEDs only, and these measurements are sent to the MTU (i.e., the SCADA server at the control center) through RTUs. The server needs these measurements to estimate the current states of the system. The resiliency requirement specify that the secured observability must be satisfied even if one IED and one RTU are unavailable (due to being suffered by technical failures or cyber attacks).

In this case of $(1, 1)$-resiliency verification, the model provides a *sat* result. That is, the system is not $(1, 1)$-resilient for secured observability, although it is $(1, 1)$-resilient observable. According to the result, if IED 3 and RTU 11 are unavailable, it is not possible to observe the system securely. There are 4 more threat vectors that can make the system unobservable. The reason is, as the result also shows, that measurements from IED 1 and RTU 9 are not data integrity protected, and as a result

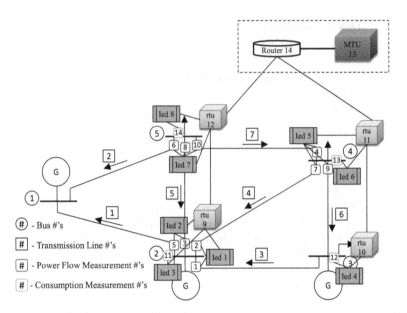

Fig. A.1 The SCADA topology of the 5-bus power grid (example scenario 2)

thus the secured observability. If the resiliency specification is reduced to $(1, 0)$ or $(0, 1)$, the model gives *unsat* result. That is, the system is securely observable even if any IED or RTU fails.

SCADA Topology 2 This scenario considers the topology shown in Fig. A.1. This SCADA topology is similar to that of Fig. 3.5, except RTU 9 is now connected with RTU 12. In this scenario, the system is not resilient any more for one RTU failures. However, there are only one threat vector (unavailability of RTU 12) to fail the secured observability.

Index

© Springer International Publishing Switzerland 2016
E. Al-Shaer, M.A. Rahman, *Security and Resiliency Analytics for Smart Grids*,
Advances in Information Security 67, DOI 10.1007/978-3-319-32871-3

Printed in the United States
By Bookmasters